2018 Taxes Made Easy

150

Questions & Answers for Individuals

Wolters Kluwer

This publication is designed to provide accurate and authoritative information in regard to the subject matter covered. It is sold with the understanding that the publisher is not engaged in rendering legal, accounting, or other professional service. If legal advice or other expert assistance is required, the services of a competent professional person should be sought.

ISBN: 978-0-8080-5184-8

No claim is made to original government works; however, within this Product or Publication, the following are subject to CCH Incorporated's copyright: (1) the gathering, compilation, and arrangement of such government materials; (2) the magnetic translation and digital conversion of data, if applicable; (3) the historical, statutory and other notes and references; and (4) the commentary and other materials.

Printed in the United States of America.

Preface

Few things produce more anxiety in people than the approach of April 15 each year. The anxiety will often begin not long after the calendar turns to a new year, and suddenly the mailbox begins to fill up with envelopes, each envelope filled with forms headed with daunting and nondescript titles, like "1099," "1098," "W-2," "1095-B" and so on. The mail stacks up on a table by the front door. Finally, around the first week of April, you decide it's time. You fire up the computer and download a couple forms off the IRS website. Then a few hours later, you decide you may as well pay for tax preparation services, because this makes no sense. If you're lucky, you just meet the deadline, either running to the Post Office with an overstuffed envelope at 11:30pm on April 15, or hurriedly typing your credit card numbers into the computer to e-file, or running to your tax preparer with a check.

Well, yeah, you've done it before, you do it every year, and it always turns out fine. You'll get it done, you always do. It wasn't so bad last year anyway. This year is going to be different. You're going to start early. So, you go get the Form 1040. Whoa! It's different! It's... shorter. Really short. But, there are new forms too? Six of them? Last year was easy. You used a 1040-EZ. You look for it. It's gone. Maybe you should just start that pile again, worry about it in April.

What happened?

At the end of 2017, Congress passed a major tax reform act, widely known as the Tax Cuts and Jobs Act. It made a lot of changes. As a result, the IRS had to do many new things, and one of the things they did was to recreate the Form 1040 to make it more usable for everyone. One main form and six new schedules. There are still several other schedules as before.

But don't panic. You can do this. Sometimes, you just need a little help. That's what this book is for—*2018 Taxes Made Easy: 150 Questions and Answers for Individuals*. It's a sort of FAQ on your Form 1040. It is organized to take you step-by-step through the new Form 1040[1] and some of the more

---

[1] The form names and line numbers referenced in this book are based upon early draft versions of the Form 1040 and Schedules available at the time of printing. The IRS may not make those forms final until closer to filing season (sometimes they procrastinate too), so you should make sure the lines referenced are correct.

significant schedules, giving a simple answer to a question you may have. It will even help as you go through your filing software. 150 questions gets you from start to finish.

It looks like this:

Adjusted Gross Income

Q What is adjusted gross income?

A Adjusted gross income is the total amount of income from compensation, ordinary dividends, retirement distributions, etc., plus any additional income such as business income, alimony, rental income, less adjustments to income (deductions available to filers regardless of whether they itemize deductions). Under the former version of the Form 1040, these adjustments to income were known as "above-the-line deductions" because they were on the front/first page of the 1040; adjusted gross income was "the line." Adjusted gross income is important to determine many income-based limitations on tax benefits, such as the medical expense deduction. Other benefits may use modified adjusted gross income, which is adjusted gross income with certain modifications that are specific to that benefit.

Okay, that was a freebie. It's 151 questions, but you'll need it later.

So, sit down with this book, make some coffee and get to work.

You can do this!

November 2018

Contents

Taxpayer Information—Form 1040

Filing Status

Q What are the different filing statuses?

A There are five filing statuses that may apply for purposes of Form 1040:

1. married filing separately;
2. single;
3. head of household;
4. married filing jointly; and
5. qualifying widow(er) with dependent child.

Q What tests must you satisfy to be considered married for filing status purposes?

A A taxpayer is generally considered married for the entire tax year if one of the following tests is satisfied on the last day of the year:

1. You and your spouse are married and living together.
2. You and your spouse are married and living apart, but you are not legally separated under a final decree of divorce or separate maintenance.
3. You and your spouse are separated under an interlocutory decree of divorce (but not under a final decree of divorce).
4. You and your spouse are living together in a common-law marriage.
5. You are considered as married at the close of the tax year if your spouse (other than a non-resident alien spouse) died during the tax year.

Q Who is treated as unmarried for filing status purposes?

A You are considered unmarried on the last day of the tax year if:

1. You are not treated as married;
2. You are legally separated from a spouse under a decree of divorce or separate maintenance; or
3. At any time during the tax year your spouse is a nonresident alien.

Q Who may file as a head of household?

A You may choose head-of-household status if:

1. You are unmarried or are considered unmarried on the last day of the tax year;
2. You paid more than half the cost of maintaining a home for the year; and
3. A "qualifying person" lived with you in the home for more than half the year.

Income—Form 1040

Wages, Salaries and Tips

Q What should I do if a Form W-2 is not provided?

A If you do not receive a Form W-2 by January 31, 2019, you should:

1. Contact your employer immediately to request the problem be corrected.
2. If your employer does not respond by February 28, contact the IRS to report the problem.
3. If the Form W-2 is not received by you in sufficient time to meet the filing deadline, a Form 1040 should be filed using a Form 4852, Substitute for Form W-2, Wage and Tax Statement, or Form 1099-R, Distributions From Pensions, Annuities, Retirement or Profit-Sharing Plans, IRAs, Insurance Contracts, etc., showing an estimate of the employee's wages for the year.

Then, if a Form W-2 is subsequently received with differing amounts, Form 1040X, Amended U.S. Individual Income Tax Return, must be filed.

Q Where do I report compensation received as an employee and what compensation is included?

A You report compensation received as an employee on Form 1040, Line 1. Such compensation includes wages, salaries, tips, and certain other forms of employee compensation.

Q How do I report tip income?

A You report tip income on Form 1040, Line 1. An employee who receives tip income in excess of $20 in a month is required to report those tips to his or her employer, including the amount distributed to other employees, and the employer will then withhold taxes for those tips from other compensation payable to the employee (if other compensation is sufficient). You should receive a W-2 from your employer that includes the amount of reported tip income, and must report that, along with any other tips not reported to your employer, on Form 1040, Line 1.

Interest

Q Where is interest income reported?

A Interest payments received during a tax year are reported on Line 2 of Form 1040, U.S. Individual Income Tax Return. Taxable interest is reported on Line 2b and tax-exempt interest is reported on Line 2a.

Q What types of interest income are reported on Form 1040?

A Interest payments received during a tax year that should be reported on Line 2b of Form 1040 include:

1. interest on bank deposits;
2. amounts paid or credited to your account by credit unions, savings and loan associations, building and loan associations, cooperative banks, mutual savings banks, and similar organizations;
3. interest on bearer certificates of deposit (CDs) and other deferred interest accounts;
4. interest on accumulated dividends paid by a life insurance company;
5. interest on delayed death benefits paid by a life insurance company;
6. interest received with damages;
7. interest on state or federal tax refunds;
8. interest on U.S. Savings Bonds, Treasury bills, Treasury bonds and Treasury notes (including Treasury inflation-protected securities);

9. interest on other indebtedness issued in registered form or of a type offered to the public, such as interest on bonds, debentures, notes, certificates and other evidence of indebtedness;
10. original issue discount (OID) on an obligation; and
11. interest on clean renewable energy bonds and Gulf tax credit bonds.

Q How is interest income from a U.S. Savings Bond reported?

A Most individual taxpayers are cash-method taxpayers (generally meaning they report income in the year received). Cash-method taxpayers can report interest income on Series E, EE, and I U.S. savings bonds under either of two methods (the chosen method must be used for all Series E, EE, and I U.S. savings bonds):

1. *Deferral Method:* Report all interest income on the bond in the earlier of (a) the tax year in which you cash in or dispose of the bond, or (b) the tax year in which the bond matures. This is the default method.
2. *Accrual Method:* Report the annual increase in the redemption value of the bond as interest income in each tax year the bond is held. This method must be elected by reporting the increase in the redemption value of the bond as interest income each year.

You can change from the deferral method to the accrual method and vice versa. It may be beneficial to switch methods to maximize the amount of reported interest income from these bonds in years where other income is lower (such as years before adulthood or years of unemployment). You can change from the deferral method to the accrual method without IRS permission, merely by reporting the accrued interest income on your tax return. You need IRS consent to change from the accrual method to the deferral method.

Q When is interest income from a U.S. Savings Bond not taxable?

A You may be able to exclude from income all or part of the interest received on the redemption of certain U.S. savings bonds if you pay qualified higher education expenses during the same tax year. U.S. savings bonds that may qualify for this treatment are Series EE bonds issued after 1989 and Series I bonds. The bond proceeds may used to pay qualified expenses of higher education for yourself, your spouse, or dependents.

To qualify for the exclusion, you must file a joint return if married, and you must be at least age 24 before the bond's issue date. The amount of the exclusion is reduced for modified adjusted gross income above $119,300 for joint returns and is completely eliminated at $149,300. For any other filing status (except for married filing separately which does not qualify) the reduction begins for modified adjusted gross income above $79,550 and is completely eliminated at $94,550.

Dividends

Q Where is dividend income reported?

A You report dividend income on Line 3 of Form 1040. Your total ordinary dividends are reported on Line 3b and any portion of those ordinary dividends that are qualified dividends are reported on Line 3a.

Q What are ordinary dividends?

A Ordinary dividends are amounts paid out of the earnings and profits of a corporation. A distribution from a corporation generally is taxable as an ordinary dividend to the extent that it does not exceed the corporation's:

1. current earnings and profits (i.e., its earnings and profits for the current tax year, as determined at the end of the current year); and
2. accumulated earnings and profits (i.e., its earnings and profits accumulated during previous tax years, as determined at the beginning of the current tax year).

Corporations generally report ordinary dividends to their shareholders on Form 1099-DIV.

Q What are qualified dividends?

A Qualified dividends are ordinary dividends that meet the following three requirements:

1. the dividends are paid by a U.S. corporation or a qualified foreign corporation;
2. you have held the stock on which the dividends were paid for a required holding period; and
3. the dividends are not one of the types of dividends that cannot be qualified dividends.

You must have held the stock on which the dividends were paid for more than 60 days during the 121-day period that begins 60 days before the ex-dividend date (the first date following the declaration of a dividend on which a buyer of the stock would not be entitled to receive the next dividend payment); or, in the case of preferred stock that had dividends due over aggregate periods of more than 366 days, you held the preferred stock on which the dividends were paid for more than 90 days during the 181-day period that begins 90 days before the ex-dividend date.

Q What types of dividends cannot be qualified dividends?

A The following types of dividends may not be treated as qualified dividends, even if they otherwise satisfy the requirements and are reported to you in Form 1099-DIV, Box 1b:

1. dividends from a corporation that is a tax-exempt organization or farmer's cooperative during the corporation's tax year in which the dividends were paid or during its previous tax year;
2. dividends paid on deposits with mutual savings banks, cooperative banks, credit unions, savings and loan associations, building and loan associations and similar financial institutions;
3. dividends paid by a corporation on employer securities that are held on the date of record by an employee stock ownership plan (ESOP) maintained by that corporation;
4. dividends paid by a regulated investment company (RIC) that are not treated as qualified dividend income;

5. dividends paid by a real estate investment trust that are not treated as qualified dividend income;

6. dividends to the extent the taxpayer is obligated (under a short sale or otherwise) to make related payments for positions in substantially similar or related property.

You must have held the stock on which the dividends were paid for more than 60 days during the 121-day period that begins 60 days before the ex-dividend date (the first date following the declaration of a dividend on which a buyer of the stock would not be entitled to receive the next dividend payment); or, in the case of preferred stock that had dividends due over aggregate periods of more than 366 days, you held the preferred stock on which the dividends were paid for more than 90 days during the 181-day period that begins 90 days before the ex-dividend date.

Q **When is a dividend declared in 2018 and paid in 2019 taxable?**

A You generally must include dividends in income in the year the payment of the dividend is actually or constructively received. Under the constructive receipt doctrine, if a dividend is declared payable in one tax year but is not actually paid until the following tax year, the dividend must be reported as income for the first tax year. However, under an exception to the constructive receipt doctrine, if a dividend is declared payable on December 31 of one tax year and the corporation follows its usual practice of mailing the dividend checks to shareholders so that they are not actually received until January of the following tax year, the dividends are not includible in income until the second tax year.

Retirement Distributions

Q **Are the distributions from a traditional IRA taxable?**

A Generally, distributions from a traditional IRA are taxable as ordinary income in the year you receive them. However, distributions from a traditional IRA that include nondeductible contributions are only partly taxable. Any part of a distribution attributable to the nondeductible contributions is not subject to tax. There are certain special rules that apply to traditional IRA distributions for taxpayers who are younger than age 59 ½ and for taxpayers who are older than age 70 ½.

Generally, if you receive a distribution from a traditional IRA before age 59 ½, there is a 10-percent additional tax that is imposed in addition to the normal tax on the distribution. And, once you reach age 70 ½, you are required to begin receiving certain minimum distributions from your traditional IRA each year. There is a 50-percent excise tax on any amount not distributed as required.

Q **What are the general tax consequences associated with IRAs?**

A Certain distributions from an IRA must be reported on Line 4 of Form 1040, U.S. Individual Income Tax Return. The taxable amount of such distributions depends on the type of IRA and certain other factors. Certain contributions to an IRA may be reported as an above-the-line deduction on Line 32 of Form 1040, Schedule 1. However, some contributions to IRAs may not be deductible.

Q **How are distributions from employer-sponsored retirement plans taxed?**

A The taxation of distributions from employer-sponsored retirement plans depends on whether:

1. pre-tax or after-tax funds were used as the source of contributions to the plan;
2. who will receive the distribution (e.g., another IRA, another qualified plan, or the taxpayer);
3. the form of the payout (e.g., lump-sum distribution or annuity payments); and
4. whether special tax treatment is available.

Distributions generally are subject to income tax at ordinary income tax rates when they are withdrawn. However, in some cases, special lump-sum taxation may be available to produce a lower tax impact. Or, if you have made after-tax contributions to the plan, then those contributions (but not the earnings on them) can be returned to you tax free. If a distribution qualifies as a tax-free rollover, then taxation is generally deferred (delayed).

Q What are the general rules that apply to payments from pensions and annuities?

A Pension and annuity payments that you receive generally must be included in your income. This includes distributions for 401(k) plans and 403(b) annuities. However, these payments do not include disability pensions you receive before reaching the minimum retirement age set by your employer or corrective distributions of excess salary deferrals or excess contributions to retirement plans.

Pension and annuity payments can include payments received from an employer-sponsored retirement plan and amounts received from an annuity outside of such a retirement plan (i.e., a commercial annuity). Pension and annuity payments are reported on Line 4 of Form 1040, U.S. Individual Income Tax Return. If all of those payments are taxable, they are only reported on 4b and 4a is left blank. If only part of the payments is taxable, the full amount is reported on 4a and the taxable amount is reported on 4b.

Social Security Benefits

Q How is the taxable amount of a lump-sum payment of Social Security benefits figured?

A Generally, a lump-sum payment is taxable based on your income for the year in which it is received. However, you may be able to reduce your tax on a lump-sum payment by electing to figure the taxable part of the lump-sum payment attributable to a prior tax year based on your income from that prior year instead of your income from the current year. Under either method, the Social Security benefits are taxable in the year they are received. The difference between the general method and the election method only affects the determination of the amount of Social Security benefits that is taxable.

If you make the lump-sum election, you must refigure the taxable part of all of your Social Security benefits for the prior tax year, including the portion of the lump-sum payment attributable to that year, by using your income for that prior year. The taxable part of the lump-sum payment attributable to that prior year is figured by subtracting the taxable part of your Social Security benefits that you previously reported for that year from the taxable part of all of you Social Security benefits for that year. The taxable amount of Social Security benefits reported for the current year is figured by adding that taxable part of his lump-sum payment that is attributable to the prior tax year to the taxable part of the lump-sum payment attributable to the current tax year (and any other payments received for the current year).

Q **What are Social Security benefits, for tax purposes?**

A Social Security benefits include monthly retirement, disability, and survivor benefits paid by the Social Security Administration under the Social Security system. Social Security benefits include tier 1 railroad retirement benefits paid by the Railroad Retirement Board. Tier 1 railroad retirement benefits are benefits that a railroad employee or beneficiary would have been entitled to receive under the Social Security system. They are considered equivalent to Social Security benefits and are treated in the same manner as Social Security benefits for tax purposes.

Q **How is the taxable amount of Social Security benefits generally figured?**

A The computation used to determine the amount of taxable Social Security benefits depends on how your modified income for the tax year compares to two specified dollar amounts, the base amount and the adjusted base amount. Your base amount ($32,000 for joint filers, $0 for married filing separately living with spouse, $25,000 all other filers) and adjusted base amount ($44,000 for joint filers, $0 for married filing separately living with spouse, $34,000 all other filers) depends on your filing status for the tax year. The method used to determine the taxation of your Social Security benefits falls into one of following three categories based on how your modified income compares to your base amount and adjusted base amount:

1. your modified income is less than your base amount;
2. your modified income is more than your base amount but less than your adjusted base amount; or
3. your modified income is more than your adjusted base amount.

Additional Income—
Schedule 1 (Form 1040)

State and Local Tax Refunds

Q How is the taxable amount of a state income tax refund generally figured?

A Generally, the full amount of a refund of state income taxes must be included in income if you deducted the state income taxes in a prior tax year. However, if you paid both state income taxes and state sales taxes and had the option of choosing to deduct one type of tax or the other, the maximum refund required to be included in income is limited to the excess of the tax you chose to deduct over the tax you did not choose to deduct.

Q How is the taxable amount of a state income tax refund figured if the taxpayer was subject to the itemized deduction limitation?

A The amount of a state income tax refund that must be included in income may be limited if you were subject to the itemized deduction limitation in the year the state income taxes were deducted. In this case, the refund is taxable only to the extent that the amount of itemized deductions allowed for that year are greater than the amount of deductions that would have been allowed for that year if itemized deductions were figured using only the net amount of the state income tax deduction (i.e., the state income tax deduction taken less the refund received). The itemized deduction limitation no longer applies to tax years begin after 2017, but would have applied to tax year 2017, and any state income tax refund received in 2018 could have been attributable to a year in which the itemized deduction limitation still applied.

Alimony Received

Q What is an alimony or separate maintenance payment?

A An alimony or separate maintenance payment is a payment that meets all of the following requirements:

1. the payment is made in cash;
2. the payment is made under a divorce or separation instrument;
3. the divorce or separation instrument does not designate the payment as non-alimony;
4. the payor-spouse is not required to make payments (or any substitute for payments) after the death of the payee-spouse;
5. if legally separated under a decree of divorce or separate maintenance, the spouses are not members of the same household at the time the payment is made; and
6. the spouses do not file a joint tax return.

Q How does a payee-spouse treat alimony or separate maintenance payments received?

A For divorce or separation agreements executed or modified prior to 2019, a spouse who receives alimony or separate maintenance payments from a spouse must include the amount received in gross income. The amount of alimony or separate maintenance payments received is reported by the payee-spouse on Line 11 of Form 1040, Schedule 1, Additional Income and Adjustments to Income. For divorce or separation agreements executed or modified after 2018, alimony is no longer included in the recipient's income.

Q When is a payor-spouse required to recapture excess alimony paid?

A Excess alimony payments are recaptured in the payor-spouse's tax year beginning in the third post-separation year by requiring the payor-spouse to include the excess in gross income that year. The payee, who previously included the payments in gross income, can deduct the amount recaptured from gross income in his or her tax year beginning in the third post-separation year. There are three steps in determining whether the recapture rule applies and, if so, the amount of excess alimony to be recaptured:

1. Determine the excess alimony paid in the second year. The excess alimony paid in the second year is the amount by which the alimony payments made in the second year exceed the sum of $15,000 plus the alimony payments made in the third year.
2. Determine the excess alimony paid in the first year. The excess alimony paid in the first year is the amount by which the alimony payments made in the first year exceed the sum of $15,000 plus the average of the alimony payments made in the second and third years. For purposes of this calculation, the alimony payments made in the second year are first reduced by the amount of the excess alimony paid in the second year (as determined in Step 1).
3. Determine the amount of excess alimony recaptured by adding together the excess alimony paid in the second year (from Step 1) and the excess alimony paid in the first year (from Step 2).

Business Income

Q How is income or loss from a business reported?

A A taxpayer who operates a business as a sole proprietor must figure income or loss from that business on Schedule C (Form 1040), Profit or Loss From Business and report it on Line 12 of Form 1040, Schedule 1, Additional Income and Adjustments to Income.

Q What expenses can be deducted by a business?

A A deduction is allowed for all ordinary and necessary expenses paid or incurred during the tax year in carrying on a trade or business. However, in order to be deductible, the expenses must be reasonable in amount. Trade or business expenses are deductible from gross income on Schedule C.

Q What method of accounting is used for a business?

A Generally, a taxpayer may choose one of the following methods of accounting:

1. the cash method;
2. an accrual method;
3. any other method permitted by the tax code and regulations; or
4. any combination of the foregoing methods, as permitted by the IRS.

Q I own an interest in an activity as a limited partner. Can I ever be treated as materially participating in the activity?

A Generally, a taxpayer who owns an interest in an activity as a limited partner is not treated as materially participating in the activity. Thus, a limited partner's distributive share of the income, gain, loss, deductions, or credits from a limited partnership activity, and any gain or loss recognized from the sale or exchange of the limited partnership interest, is generally presumed to be passive.

However, a limited partner who meets the 500-hour test, the five-of-ten-preceding-years test, or the personal service activity test is treated as materially participating in such an activity.

Q What types of activities are considered passive activities?

A The following two types of activities are passive activities:

1. a trade or business activity in which you do not materially participate; and
2. a rental activity.

Q Can losses disallowed as a result of the at-risk rules be deducted in the following year?

A Any loss disallowed due to the at-risk limitations may be carried over and deducted in the following year, subject to application of the at-risk limitations in that year. There is no limit on the number of years to which you may carry over such a loss.

Q For what amounts am I considered at risk?

A You are at risk in an activity for the following amounts:

1. the money and adjusted basis of property contributed by you to the activity; and
2. any amount you borrow for use in the activity, to the extent you are personally liable for the repayment of the loan or have pledged property (other than property used in the activity) as security for the loan.

Capital Gains

Q Are capital losses deductible?

A The deductibility of capital losses is severely restricted. Capital losses generally are deductible only to the extent of capital gains, but individual taxpayers may also deduct $3,000 of the excess of aggregate capital losses (either long term or short term) over aggregate capital gains (either long term or short term) against ordinary income. The amount of any remaining capital loss that is not deductible is referred to as a net capital loss.

Q What is a capital asset?

A A capital asset is any property held by you (whether or not connected with your trade or business) other than the following types of property:

1. stock in trade, inventory, and property held primarily for sale to customers;
2. depreciable or real property used in a trade or business;
3. copyrights and certain property created by your own efforts;
4. accounts or notes receivable;
5. certain government publications;
6. commodities derivative financial instruments held by commodities derivative dealers, other than those that are identified as having no connection to the activities of the dealer as a dealer;
7. hedging transactions; and
8. supplies of a type regularly used or consumed by you in the ordinary course of your trade or business.

Q **What tax rates apply to net capital gains?**

A If you have a net capital gain, your long-term capital gains and losses must be separated into three maximum tax rate groups: (1) the 28-percent group; (2) the 25-percent group; and (3) the 15-percent group.

The 28-percent group consists of capital gains and losses from collectibles (including works of art, rugs, antiques, metals, gems, stamps, coins, and alcoholic beverages) held for more than one year, but only to the extent such gain is taken into account in computing gross income and such loss is taken into account in computing taxable income. The 28 percent group also includes an amount equal to the gain excluded under the rules relating to the sale of small business stock.

The 25-percent group consists of unrecaptured Code Sec. 1250 gain —there are no losses in this group. Unrecaptured Code Sec. 1250 gain is long-term capital gain, not otherwise recaptured as ordinary income, attributable to prior depreciation of real property.

The 15-percent group consists of long-term capital gains and losses that are from sales or exchanges of property that are not in the 28-percent or 25-percent group. For purposes of applying these rates, net capital gain is increased by the amount of your qualified dividend income.

Q **Is my long-term capital gain from the sale of property and qualified dividend income taxed at 0, 15, or 20 percent?**

A For long-term capital gain from the sale of property (not in the 28 or 25-percent group) and qualified dividends, a rate of 0, 15, or 20 percent may apply. The determination of the applicable rate depends upon your filing status and total taxable income. For 2018, the zero-percent rate applies to long-term capital gains and qualified dividends for joint filers with taxable income below $77,200; heads of household below $51,700, unmarried taxpayers and married taxpayers filing separately below $38,600, and estates and trusts below $2,600. The 20-percent rate applies to joint filers with taxable income of at least $479,000, heads of household with at least $452,400, unmarried taxpayers with at least $425,800, married taxpayers filing separately with at least $239,500, and estates and trusts with at least $12,700. The 15-percent rate applies to taxpayers between the two "breakpoints."

Sale of a Home

Q If I qualify, what is the maximum amount of gain that I may exclude on the sale of a principal residence?

A Under the rules for the exclusion of gain on the sale of a principal residence, you generally can exclude up to $250,000 ($500,000 for married taxpayers filing jointly) of any gain on the sale of the principal residence.

Q What are the ownership and residency requirements to qualify for the exclusion of gain from a sale of a home?

A You may claim the full amount of the exclusion only if you owned and used the home as a principal residence for an aggregate of at least two of the five years before its sale. The ownership-and-use test is satisfied by establishing ownership and use either for 24 full months or for 730 days (365 days × 2 years). The two years of ownership and use need not be continuous and they need not be concurrent. All that is required is that the home is owned for an aggregate of two years during the five-year period before the date of sale and that the home is used as a principal residence for an aggregate of two years during the five-year period before the date of sale. Married taxpayers who file a joint return for the tax year of the sale meet the ownership and use test if either spouse meets these requirements.

Q Do I currently have to live in the principal residence to qualify for the exclusion of gain from a sale of a home?

A The home that is sold does not have to be your principal residence at the time of purchase or sale—all that is required to meet the ownership and use test is that you used the home as a principal residence for a total of two years or more during the five-year period before the date of sale. For example, you could move from your principal residence into your vacation home and then have up to three more years to sell your principal residence and claim the exclusion.

Q **Do the ownership and use tests for the principal residence exclusion apply to people outside the country?**

A The five-year period for determining the ownership and use of a home may be suspended at your election during a period of time that either you or your spouse spouse are:

1. serving on qualified official extended duty as a member of the uniformed services, a member of the U.S. Foreign Service, or as a specified employee of the intelligence community; or
2. serving outside the United States on qualified official extended duty as an employee of the Peace Corps or as an enrolled volunteer or volunteer leader under section 5 or 6 of the Peace Corps Act.

Qualified official extended duty is any extended duty while serving at a duty station that is at least 50 miles from your home or while residing in government quarters under government orders. Extended duty is a period of active duty pursuant to a call or order to such duty for a period in excess of 90 days or for an indefinite period. The suspension of the five-year period may not be extended for more than ten years. The election to suspend the five-year period may not be made for your home if you have such an election in effect on another home. However, an election on a home may be revoked at any time.

Q **Do the ownership and use tests apply if a home sale is due to health or work-related issues?**

A If you do not meet the two-year ownership and use test for the exclusion of gain on the sale of a principal residence, you are not eligible for the full exclusion of $250,000 (or $500,000 if married filing jointly). However, you may be eligible for a reduced exclusion in certain hardship situations. The reduced exclusion is available if you sell your principal residence because of a change in place of employment, health, or certain unforeseen circumstances. The reduced exclusion is computed by multiplying the full exclusion amount of $250,000 ($500,000 if married filing jointly) by a fraction, the numerator of which is the shortest of:

1. the period of time that you owned the home during the five-year period ending on the date of the sale;
2. the period of time that you used the home as your principal residence during the five-year period ending on the date of the sale; or
3. the period of time between the date of any prior sale of a principal residence for which you claimed an exclusion and the date of the current sale.

The denominator of the fraction is 730 days or 24 months (depending on the measure of time used in the numerator).

Q **If I own two homes, which home is considered the principal residence?**

A If you have more than one home, the determination of which home is the principal residence is made based on all the facts and circumstances. If a you alternate between two homes, using each home for successive periods of time, the home that you use a majority of the time during the year is ordinarily considered your principal residence.

Sales and Exchanges

Q **When is gain determined under the installment method?**

A When a you dispose of property for which at least one payment is to be received after the close of the tax year, any gain from the disposition is determined under the installment method.

Caution: A loss on an installment sale cannot be reported under the installment method. Instead, the loss is deductible only in the tax year of the sale.

Q Can I out of the installment method?

A You can elect out of the installment method. The election can be made for any disposition in a tax year for which the installment method would otherwise apply. If the election is made, the entire gain is taxed in the year of disposition. The election must be made on or before the due date, including extensions, for filing your return for the year in which the sale is made.

Q What types of property qualify for like-kind exchange treatment?

A After 2017, both properties in a like-kind exchange must be real property (i.e., real estate) held for productive use in a trade or business or for investment to qualify for like-kind exchange treatment. Prior to 2018, a like-kind exchange applied to personal, as well as real, property.

Q When is gain or loss recognized on a like-kind exchange?

A Gain or loss in a like-kind exchange is recognized if, in addition to the new like-kind property, other property or money (so-called boot) is received. The recipient's gain is recognized up to the amount of any money received or fair market value of any other property received. No loss is recognized on the exchange, except for a loss on other property exchanged if, on the exchange date, the adjusted basis of the non-like-kind property is greater than the fair market value of such property.

Q What requirements must be met for property to be considered involuntarily converted?

A The conversion of the property must result from the destruction of the property (in whole or in part), the theft of the property, a governmental taking of the property through seizure, a governmental taking of the property through condemnation or requisition, or the threat or imminence of such a condemnation or requisition.

Q **Is gain recognized when property is involuntarily converted into property that is not similar or related in service or use to the converted property?**

A If property is involuntarily converted into money or other property that is not similar or related in service or use to the converted property, you must recognize the entire amount of gain realized on the involuntary conversion unless:

1. you elect to defer recognition of a portion of the gain (i.e., to recognize gain only to the extent that the amount realized upon the conversion exceeds the cost of replacement property or stock); and
2. within a specified time period, you acquire property similar or related in service or use to the converted property, or stock that gives you a controlling interest in a corporation that owns property similar or related in service or use to the converted property.

Q **What is the effect of an involuntary conversion (i.e., destruction, taking or condemnation) of a residence?**

A An involuntary conversion of a principal residence by destruction, theft, seizure, condemnation, or requisition is treated as a sale. Thus, the exclusion of gain on the sale of a principal residence is taken into account in determining the amount realized on its involuntary conversion. The amount realized on the conversion is the amount determined without regard to the principal residence exclusion, reduced by the amount of gain excluded. The owner's holding period and use of the converted property carries over to a replacement home.

Q **What are the below-market loan rules?**

A The below-market loan rules apply only if a loan does not provide sufficient interest. A loan provides sufficient interest only if the interest charged equals or exceeds the appropriate applicable federal rate. There are potential tax consequences for both the lender and borrower of a below-market loan.

Q What types of loans are affected by the below-market loan rules?

A The loans affected by the below-market loan rules are:

1. gift loans;
2. compensation-related loans;
3. corporation-shareholder loans;
4. tax avoidance loans;
5. other below-market loans; and
6. loans to qualified continuing care facilities.

Other Gains and Losses

Q What other gains and losses are generally reported on Line 14 of Form 1040, Schedule 1?

A You must report on Form 1040, Line 14, gains and losses from the sale or exchange of assets used in a trade or business. These gains and losses are generally reported on Form 4797, Sales of Business Property, and carried over to Form 1040.

Q What types of property are subject to these rules for other gains and losses?

A Code Sec. 1231 applies to gain or loss recognized on the sale or exchange or the involuntary conversion of property used in a trade or business as well as to the involuntary conversion of capital assets held for more than one year. For this purpose, property used in a trade or business may include real property and depreciable property that the taxpayer has held for more than one year. Only property held by the taxpayer for more than one year qualifies for Code Sec. 1231 treatment. The holding period is calculated in the same manner as the holding period for characterizing capital gains and losses.

Note that the following assets are not considered Code Sec. 1231 property:

1. inventory, stock-in-trade, and property held primarily for sale to customers in the ordinary course of your trade or business;
2. copyrights, literary, musical, or artistic compositions and similar property either created by your own efforts or acquired by gift or transfer in trust;
3. letters, memoranda, and similar property held by the author, donees of the author, or persons to whom they were sent or for whom they were produced; and
4. publications of the U.S. government that you receive from the government at a price less than that offered to the general public.

Q **How are these other gains and losses calculated?**

A The character of gain or loss under Code Sec. 1231 depends on whether your Code Sec. 1231 gains exceed your Code Sec. 1231 losses for the year. If your Code Sec. 1231 gains exceed your Code Sec. 1231 losses, all of your Code Sec. 1231 gains and losses are treated as long-term capital gains and losses (subject to certain recapture provisions). These amounts are taken into account along with your other capital gains and losses for the year. If your Code Sec. 1231 losses equal or exceed your Code Sec. 1231 gains, all of your Code Sec. 1231 gains and losses are treated as ordinary.

Any gain required by Code Sec. 1245 or Code Sec. 1250 to be recaptured as ordinary income is not Code Sec. 1231 gain. Conversely, any gain on the sale that is not subject to recapture is Code Sec. 1231 gain. Any amount required by Code Sec. 1239 (relating to gain from sale of depreciable property between certain related taxpayers) to be treated as ordinary income is also not Code Sec. 1231 gain.

Rental Real Estate, Royalties, Income From Passthrough Entities

Q What is the tax treatment of a personal residence rented for 15 days or more during the year?

A If a dwelling unit is a personal residence you rent it for 15 days or more during the tax year, then the rental income generated is recognized as taxable income. You may deduct any related rental expenses incurred. However, in this case, the amount of the deduction for rental expenses is limited to the amount of gross rental income generated by the dwelling unit.

Q What is the tax treatment of a personal residence rented for less than 15 days during the year?

A If a dwelling unit is a personal residence and you rent it for less than 15 days during the tax year, then the rental income generated is not recognized as taxable income. The related rental expenses incurred are not deductible. You may, however, deduct allowable mortgage interest, real estate taxes, and casualty losses related to the property if you itemize your deductions on Form 1040, Schedule A.

Q When is a home treated as a personal residence for purposes of the rental income rules?

A A dwelling unit is treated as your personal residence during the year if you make personal use of the dwelling unit for a number of days that exceeds the greater of:

1. 14 days; or
2. 10 percent of the number of days during the year for which the unit is rented at a fair rental.

Q **What are royalties?**

A Royalties are payments you receive for permitting someone else to use your property. Royalties are commonly received for the use of your intangible rights. Royalties are also often received for the right to exploit the natural resources on your property.

Q **How are royalties reported on my return?**

A Royalty income is often reported on Form 1040, U.S. Individual Income Tax Return Schedule E, Supplemental Income and Loss. The gross amount of royalties is reported on Line 4 of Schedule E. Any taxes withheld from the royalties are reported on Line 16 of Schedule E. The net amount of royalty income or loss from Schedule E is reported on Form 1040, Schedule 1, Line 17.

Amounts on Schedule E are carried over to Form 1040, but are not included on Schedule SE, Self-employment Tax, in calculating self-employment tax. However, if you hold an operating oil, gas, or mineral interest or are in business as a self-employed writer, inventor, artist, etc., royalty income is reported on Form 1040, Schedule C, Profit or Loss from Business, and is subject to self-employment tax.

Q **How does a partner treat distributions received from a partnership?**

A If a partner receives a distribution of money or marketable securities in excess of the partner's basis in his partnership interest, the partner generally reports the excess as capital gain. During the year, a partner first increases his basis by his allocable share of partnership income, contributions, or increases in the partnership's liabilities, then reduces his basis for distributions received during the year. However, if a partnership has a loss, a partner reduces his basis by the amount of the distributions before deducting any losses. This ordering rule may cause losses to be suspended due to a lack of basis.

Q I am a partner. Can I deduct my share of a partnership loss?

A Determining whether you can deduct your share of a partnership loss is a multi-step process:

Step 1: Determine whether you have sufficient basis. In addition to determining whether you have a positive or negative capital account, you must consider whether there are any differences between the inside and outside basis. Note that for purposes of determining your basis, your distributive share of all liabilities is added to the tax basis capital account, regardless of whether the liabilities are recourse, non-recourse, or qualified non-recourse.

Step 2: Determine at-risk limitations. Non-recourse liabilities typically do not provide at-risk basis. Therefore, in determining whether you have sufficient amounts at risk to be able to deduct the loss, the non-recourse liabilities normally are disregarded. There is an exception for partners in real estate partnerships who acquired their partnership interest before 1987. The at-risk rules do not apply to partners falling within this exception.

Step 3: Determine if losses are subject to the passive activity loss limitations. Even if a partner has both tax basis and sufficient amounts at risk to deduct a loss, if the losses are passive in nature, they may not be deductible under the passive activity loss rules. Whether a loss is passive is determined at the partner level, taking into account such factors as whether the activity is a rental, the level of the partner's involvement in the activity, and the type of ownership interest (general, limited, or LLC member).

Farm Income or Loss

Q What types of farm income are reported on Schedule F of a farmer's return?

A A farmer reports farm income in either Part I or Part III of Schedule F, depending on whether he is a cash method farmer or an accrual method farmer. The types of income that generally must be reported on Schedule F include:

1. amounts received from the sale of livestock, produce, grains, and other products that are raised for sale or bought for resale;
2. distributions from cooperatives, including patronage dividends and per-unit retain certificates;
3. payments from governmental agricultural programs;
4. the loan proceeds from Commodity Credit Corporation (CCC) loans secured by crops or another commodity (included in income at the taxpayer's election);
5. crop insurance proceeds received as a result of crop damage, including crop disaster payments received from the federal government;
6. amounts received for custom hire work and machine work; and
7. other types of income, including gains and losses from hedging transactions.

Q What types of farm expenses can I deduct on Schedule F of a farmer's return?

A Deductible farming expenses are reported on Schedule F, Part II, which lists many types of expenses that are common to farming operations. Generally, as a farmer, you may deduct the ordinary and necessary costs of operating a farm for profit as business expenses. There are some deduction rules that are unique to farming. A farmer can deduct certain expenses for soil conservation or for the prevention of erosion of land used for farming. However, such deductions are limited to 25 percent of the farmer's gross income from farming.

Note that, for other taxpayers, these types of expenses generally must be capitalized and added to the basis of the land. There are certain other rules unique to farming. These include the limitation of a deduction for the costs of prepaid farm supplies and livestock feed, the denial of a deduction for certain farm costs that must be capitalized or included in inventory, and the special recordkeeping rules that apply to farm vehicles.

Unemployment Compensations

Q What payments are treated as unemployment compensation?

A The following types of benefits are considered unemployment compensation, and reported on Form 1040, Schedule 1, Additional Income and Adjustments to Income, Line 19:

1. state unemployment insurance benefits;
2. benefits paid by a state from the Federal Unemployment Trust Fund;
3. railroad unemployment compensation benefits;
4. disability payments from a government program paid as a substitute for unemployment compensation;
5. unemployment assistance paid under the Disaster Relief and Emergency Assistance Act of 1974;
6. Trade Readjustment Allowances paid under the Trade Act of 1974; and
7. Unemployment assistance under the Airline Deregulation Act of 1978 Program.

Q How should I treat unemployment compensation when I have made prior nondeductible contributions to a government unemployment compensation program?

A If you made nondeductible contributions to a government unemployment compensation program, benefits received under the program are reported as unemployment compensation, but only to the extent that they exceed the amount of the your contributions.

Q How should I treat unemployment compensation that is repaid?

A If your received unemployment compensation in 2018 and part of the amount received is then repaid in 2018, you report the net amount received on Form 1040, Schedule 1, Additional Income and Adjustments to Income, Line 19. On the dotted line next to Line 19, write "repaid" and the dollar amount that is repaid.

If unemployment compensation was received and included in income in a year before 2018 and then repaid during 2018, the reporting treatment depends on the amount repaid. If the amount you repaid was $3,000 or less, it may be deducted on Schedule A, Itemized Deductions, as a tax deduction. If the amount you repaid was more than $3,000 and you had an unrestricted right to the unemployment compensation in the year received, you can take either a deduction or a credit for the repayment amount. You should figure your tax under both methods to determine which method results in lower tax. Note that you must itemize deductions on Schedule A in order to take a deduction for a repayment.

Other Income

Q How is the taxable portion of a distribution from a Coverdell education savings account (ESA) calculated?

A Distributions out of the ESA are assumed to include pro rata portions of principal (i.e., contributions) and earnings. The portion of the distribution allocable to principal generally is not taxable. For purposes of measuring the taxability of the earnings portion of the distribution, qualified education expenses are compared to the total distribution (not just the earnings portion of the distribution). If qualified education expenses equal or exceed the total distribution, then the income is fully excludable. Otherwise, the amount of the earnings portion of the distribution that is excludable is equal to the earnings portion of the distribution multiplied by the ratio of qualified education expenses to the total distribution. The taxable portion is reported on Form 1040, Schedule 1, Additional Income and Adjustments to Income, Line 21.

Q How is the taxable portion of a distribution from a qualified tuition program (QTP) calculated?

A Distributions out of a QTP are assumed to include pro rata portions of contributions and earnings. The portion of the distribution allocable to principal (i.e., contributions) generally is not taxable. For purposes of measuring the taxability of the earnings portion of the distribution, qualified education expenses are compared to the total distribution (not just the income portion of the distribution). If qualified education expenses equal or exceed the total distribution, then the income is fully excludable. Otherwise, the amount of the earnings portion of the distribution that is excludable is equal to the earnings portion of the distribution multiplied by the ratio of qualified education expenses to the total distribution. The taxable portion is reported on Form 1040, Schedule 1, Additional Income and Adjustments to Income, Line 21.

Q How is a court award taxed and reported?

A If you receive settlement amounts by judgment or compromise, the taxability of the settlement amounts received depends on the nature of the underlying claim. Compensatory damages for personal physical injury or physical sickness generally are not taxable. Compensatory damages for emotional distress may be taxable if the emotional distress is not due to a personal physical injury or physical sickness. Punitive damages are generally taxable. Legal fees recovered from the other party are taxable if the underlying settlement amounts are taxable. Taxable court awards are reported on Form 1040, Schedule 1, Additional Income and Adjustments to Income, Line 21.

Q How is a canceled debt taxed and reported?

A If you are personally liable for a debt and the debt is canceled or forgiven by the lender, you generally must include the amount of the canceled debt in income. This amount is known as cancellation of debt (COD) income. If it involves a nonbusiness debt, it is generally reported as other income on Form 1040, Schedule 1, Additional Income and Adjustments to Income, Line 21. If it involves a business debt, the reporting depends on the type of business debt involved. It is generally reported on Form 1040, Schedule C if related to a sole proprietorship, Schedule E if related to a rental activity, or Schedule F if related to a farming business.

Q How are gambling winnings (or losses) taxed and reported?

A Gambling winnings may be offset by gambling losses (including, for 2018 through 2025, any normal expenses incurred in engaging in gambling activities). However, gambling winnings and losses must be reported separately. Netting is not allowed. Gambling losses that exceed gambling winnings are not deductible, even if you are a professional gambler. On a joint return, gambling losses of one spouse may offset winnings of the other spouse.

Gambling winnings may be reported to you on Form W-2G, and may be subject to withholding. Gambling winnings are generally reported as other income on Form 1040, Schedule 1, Additional Income and Adjustments to Income, Line 21. Gambling losses are normally treated as a miscellaneous itemized deduction."

Q How is jury duty pay taxed and reported?

A Jury duty pay must be reported as other income on Form 1040, Schedule 1, Additional Income and Adjustments to Income, Line 21.

Nontaxable Items

Items Not Generally Reported on a Form

Q Can I exclude payments from my employer for dependent care assistance?

A An employee can exclude from gross income amounts that his or her employer pays or incurs for dependent care assistance furnished to the employee under a qualified dependent care assistance program. However, the amount that can be excluded for such dependent care assistance is subject to several limitations:

1. the amount that can be excluded is limited to $5,000 ($2,500 if married filing separately) for each tax year; and
2. the amount that can be excluded is limited to the lower of: (a) the earned income of the employee, or (b) the earned income of the employee's spouse.

Q Can I exclude amounts related to accident and health insurance plans?

A Generally, a taxpayer may exclude from gross income amounts received through accident or health insurance for personal injuries or sickness. If you receive such amounts as an employee, you may exclude them if they:

1. reimburse you for medical expenses incurred for medical care for him of you, your spouse or a dependent; or
2. the amount that can be excluded is limited to the lower of: (a) your earned income, or (b) the earned income of your spouse.

You may exclude from gross income the amount of any contributions your employer makes to an accident or health plan in order to compensate you (through insurance or otherwise) for personal injuries or sickness incurred by you, your spouse, or dependents.

Q Can I exclude amounts paid by my employer
for my education?

A You can exclude from gross income amounts that your employer pays
or incurs for educational assistance furnished to you under a qualified
educational assistance program. However, the amount that can be
excluded for such educational assistance is limited to $5,250 for each
calendar year. Educational assistance eligible for the exclusion includes:

1. the payment of expenses incurred for your education, including
   tuition, fees, books, supplies and equipment; and
2. the provision of courses of instruction for you, including books,
   supplies and equipment.

Q Can I exclude amounts paid by an employer
for adoptions?

A You can exclude from gross income amounts that your employer pays
or incurs for adoption assistance furnished to you under an adoption
assistance program. However, the amount that can be excluded for such
adoption assistance is subject to several limitations:

1. the amount that can be excluded for such adoption assistance in
   2018 is limited to $13,810 of qualified adoption expenses; and
2. the amount that can be excluded is phased out for taxpayers with 2018
   modified adjusted gross income between $207,140 and $247,140.

Q What employee fringe benefits can be excluded from income?

A You may exclude from gross income certain fringe benefits provided by
your employer. These include:

1. **No additional cost fringe benefits.** This exclusion applies whether
   the service is provided either without charge or at a reduced price,
   and whether it is provided either directly or through a cash rebate
   of all or part of any amount paid for the service.
2. **Employee Discounts.** You can exclude from gross income a
   fringe benefit that qualifies as a qualified employee discount. This

exclusion applies whether the property or service is either provided without charge or at a reduced price, and whether it is provided either directly or through a cash rebate of all or part of any amount paid for the service.

3. **Working condition fringe benefits.** You can exclude a working condition fringe benefit from gross income. A working condition fringe benefit is any property or service provided to you to the extent that you would have been allowed a trade or business expense deduction or a depreciation deduction if you had paid for the property or service.

4. *De minimis* **fringe benefits.** You can exclude a *de minimis* fringe benefit from gross income. A *de minimis* fringe benefit is any property or service the value of which is so small as to make accounting for it unreasonably or administratively impracticable.

Q Is an employer-provided cell phone taxable to me?

A If an employer provides a cell phone primarily for noncompensatory business reasons, the IRS will treat your use of the cell phone for business reasons as a working condition fringe benefit, and the business and personal use of the cell phone as generally nontaxable to you. An employer will be considered to have provided you with a cell phone primarily for noncompensatory business purposes if there are substantial reasons relating to the employer's business, other than providing compensation to you, for providing you with a cell phone.

Q Can I exclude payments from my employer for transportation to work?

A For 2018, you can exclude from gross income a fringe benefit that qualifies as a qualified transportation fringe benefit. Qualified transportation fringe benefits include:

1. transportation provided in a commuter highway vehicle;
2. any transit pass; and
3. qualified parking.

For 2018, the amount of qualified transportation fringe benefits that may be excluded is limited to:

1. in the case of the aggregate value of transit passes and transportation provided in a commuter highway vehicle, $260 per month; and
2. in the case of the value of qualified parking, $260 per month.

Q Is a forgiven mortgage taxable to me?

A Generally, a cancelation of debt is taxable, and the amount of the canceled debt is included as income. However, where a canceled debt is qualified principle residence indebtedness (i.e., a mortgage), an exclusion may apply. The exclusion has to be renewed by an act of Congress to apply to mortgages forgiven in 2018, so taxpayers should confirm the exclusion is available before excluding it from income.

Adjustments to Income— Schedule 1 (Form 1040)

Educator Expenses

Q May I claim the deduction for educator expenses?

A The deduction for educator expenses is only available to an eligible educator. For this purpose, an eligible educator is a taxpayer who is a teacher, instructor, counselor, principal or aide who works for at least 900 hours during the school year at a school that provides elementary or secondary education. Elementary or secondary education is education provided to students in kindergarten through grade 12.

Q What expenses qualify for the deduction for educator expenses?

A The deduction for educator expenses is only available for qualified expenses. Qualified expenses include the expenses of books, supplies, equipment and supplementary materials used in the classroom. For this purpose, equipment includes computer equipment and related software and services.

Certain Business Expenses of Reservists, Performing Artists, and Fee-Basis Government Officials

Q What expenses may a qualified performing artist deduct?

A A performing artist may deduct his employee business expenses if the following requirements are met:

1. the performing artist performed services in the performing arts as an employee of more than one employer during the tax year;

2. the performing artist received wages of at least $200 per employer from more than one of those employers during the tax year;
3. the business expenses attributable to performing arts services performed during the tax year were more than 10 percent of the gross income from those performing arts services; and
4. the performing artist's adjusted gross income (AGI) for the tax year was $16,000 or less, before the deduction of such business expenses.

Q What expenses may a reservist deduct?

A A member of a reserve component of the U.S. Armed Forces may deduct travel expenses if the member travels more than 100 miles away from home in connection with the performance of services as a reservist. However, this above-the-line deduction is limited by the travel expense rates that apply to U.S. government employees.

Q What expenses may a fee-based government employee deduct?

A A governmental official may deduct his or her employee business expenses if the official:

1. is employed by a state or local government (or by a political subdivision of such a government); and
2. is compensated on a fee basis, in whole or in part.

The amount of employee business expenses deductible is the amount attributable to the expenses the government official incurred for services performed in that job.

Health Savings Accounts (HSAs)

Q **Can I deduct contributions to a health savings account (HSA)?**

A You generally can deduct contributions to an HSA if:

1. you are covered under a high deductible health plan (HDHP); and
2. you are not covered under any other health plan that is not an HDHP. An HDHP is a health plan that has a specified minimum annual deductible and a specified maximum annual out-of-pocket expense.

You cannot deduct HSA contributions if you may be claimed as a dependent on another taxpayer's return. You are also not eligible to deduct HSA contributions that are made after enrolling in Medicare.

Q **Is there any limitation on the amount of the health savings account (HSA) deduction?**

A There is a limitation on the amount of HSA contributions that may be deducted. The limitation amount depends on whether you have self-only (limit for 2018 is $3,450) or family coverage (limit for 2018 is $6,850). If you turn age 55 before the end of the tax year, the maximum deductible contribution amount is increased by a $1,000 "catch-up contribution" amount.

Moving Expenses

Q **When can moving expenses be deducted?**

A For 2018, moving expenses are only deductible for members of the U.S. Armed Forces on active duty moving to a new station. You need not satisfy tests related to time in prior location or the distance between the new post and new home relative to the old home in order to take the deduction.

Self-Employment Tax Deduction

Q Where do I figure the self-employment tax deduction?

A The self-employment tax and deduction for self-employment tax are both figured on Schedule SE (Form 1040), Self-Employment Tax. The deduction is then reported on Line 27 of Form 1040, Schedule 1, Additional Income and Adjustments to Income. (The self-employment tax from Schedule SE is reported on Line 57 of Form 1040, Schedule 4, Other Taxes.)

Self-Employed Retirement Plans

Q Which self-employed persons are eligible for the deduction for self-employed SEP, SIMPLE, and qualified plans?

A A self-employed taxpayer is a person who has self-employment income during the tax year. Self-employment income consists of the net earnings derived from a trade or business carried on as a sole proprietor or by a partnership of which he is a member.

Q What contributions can a self-employed taxpayer deduct?

A A self-employed taxpayer may take a deduction for contributions made to the following types of retirement plans:

1. a Simplified Employee Pension (SEP) plan;
2. a Savings Incentive Match Plan for Employees (SIMPLE); or
3. a qualified plan.

Self-Employed Health Insurance Deduction

Q Can I take the self-employed health insurance deduction?

A The deduction for self-employed health insurance premiums may be taken if you are:

1. A self-employed individual with a net profit for the tax year.
2. A partner with net earnings from self-employment.
3. An S corporation shareholder who owns more than 2 percent of the outstanding stock of the S corporation and has wages from the S corporation.

However, the deduction is not available for any month during which you were eligible to participate in any employer-subsidized health plan maintained by your employer or your spouse's employer.

Q What types of insurance are eligible for the self-employed health insurance deduction?

A The deduction may be taken only for premiums paid for medical insurance, dental insurance and qualified long-term care insurance. Moreover, the deduction may be taken only for premiums for insurance that covers you, your spouse and dependents. The premiums paid for medical insurance and dental insurance are fully deductible. However, the amount of the deduction for qualified long-term care insurance premiums is subject to limitations based on the year-end age of the persons covered.

Penalty on Early Withdrawal of Savings

Q What amounts qualify for the deduction of the penalty for the early withdrawal of savings?

A The deduction for a penalty on the early withdrawal of savings is allowed for amounts forfeited to a financial institution as a penalty for the premature withdrawal of funds from a time-savings account, certificate of deposit, or similar class of deposit. These types of accounts are generally referred to as deferred interest accounts.

Q How do I determine the amount of my penalties on the early withdrawal of savings?

A The amount of any penalties paid by you for the early withdrawal of funds from a deferred interest account are reported to you by the financial institution on Form 1099-INT, Interest Income, or Form 1099-OID, Original Issue Discount. On Form 1099-INT, the financial institution reports the gross amount of interest income paid or credited to you for the year in Box 1 and the amount of any early withdrawal penalties that are charged to you in Box 2.

On Form 1099-OID, the financial institution reports the amount of original issue discount in Box 1, the amount of other periodic interest income in Box 2, and the amount of any early withdrawal penalties that are charged to you in Box 3. Thus, the financial institution calculates the amount of any penalties and reports them to you. You may take a deduction for the aggregate amounts of early withdrawal penalties reported to you by financial institutions in Box 2 of Forms 1099-INT and Box 3 of Forms 1099-OID.

Alimony Paid

Q Who qualifies to take the deduction for alimony paid?

A A taxpayer who pays alimony or separate maintenance payments to a spouse may take a deduction for the amount paid. The deduction for alimony or separate maintenance payments is treated as an above-the-line deduction in computing adjusted gross income. The deduction is only available for divorce or separation instruments executed or modified before 2019. The amount of alimony or separate maintenance paid is reported as a deduction on Line 31 of Form 1040, Schedule 1, Additional Income and Adjustments to Income.

Q What payments are eligible for the deduction for alimony paid?

A An alimony or separate maintenance payment is a payment that meets all of the following requirements:

1. the payment is made in cash;
2. the payment is made under a divorce or separation instrument;
3. the divorce or separation instrument does not designate the payment as non-alimony;
4. the payor-spouse is not required to make payments (or any substitute for payments) after the death of the payee-spouse;
5. if legally separated under a decree of divorce or separate maintenance, the spouses are not members of the same household at the time the payment is made; and
6. the spouses do not file a joint tax return.

Caution: The deduction is only available for divorce or separation instruments executed or modified before 2019.

Individual Retirement Account Contributions

Q Are there limitations on deducting contributions to a traditional IRA?

A Generally, you can deduct contributions made to a traditional IRA up to the amount of the contribution limitations. The amount of a the deduction for contributions to a traditional IRA may be subject to an additional limitation if you or your spouse was covered by an employer retirement plan at any time during the year for which the contributions were made.

Q Who is covered by an employer retirement plan?

A A taxpayer generally is considered to be covered by an employer retirement plan if the "Retirement Plan" box on his or her Form W-2, Wage and Tax Statement, from the employer is checked. If in doubt, you should check with your employer. However, you are not considered to be covered by an employer retirement plan merely because you:

1. have coverage under Social Security or railroad retirement;
2. receives retirement benefits from a previous employer's plan;
3. participates in the plan because you are a member of a reserve unit of the armed forces; or
4. participate in the plan because you are a volunteer firefighter.

Q How do the rules for Roth IRAs differ from the rules for traditional IRAs?

A A Roth IRA is subject to many of the same rules as a traditional IRA. However, there are some important differences in the rules that apply to the two types of IRAs. There is no maximum age limit for setting up and contributing to a Roth IRA. The contributions to a Roth IRA are never deductible. The distributions from a Roth IRA are not taxable if certain requirements are met. And, there is no requirement that you begin receiving distributions from a Roth IRA by a certain age.

Student Loan Interest Deduction

Q What interest qualifies for the student loan interest deduction?

A You may deduct interest paid during the tax year on a qualified education loan. However, this student loan interest deduction is subject to certain limitations. The maximum deduction is $2,500, but is reduced or eliminated for filers with adjusted gross income above $65,000 ($135,000 for joint filers).

Q What are qualified education loans?

A A qualified education loan is a loan incurred solely to pay qualified higher education expenses that are attributable to education furnished during an academic period in which the recipient was an eligible student. There are several additional qualified education loan requirements regarding the permitted recipients of the qualified higher education expenses and the timing of the payment of those expenses. A loan used solely to refinance one or more qualified education loans may also be a qualified education loan. A loan does not have to be issued or guaranteed under a federal postsecondary education loan program to be a qualified education loan. However, some types of loans may not be qualified education loans, even if they otherwise satisfy the requirements.

Tuition and Fees Deduction

Q Can I take the tuition and fees deduction?

A You may take the tuition and fees deduction for tax years in which the deduction is available, if you pay qualified education expenses for you, your spouse, or a dependent who you can claim on your tax return. The person for whom the expenses are paid must be an eligible student enrolled at or attending an eligible educational institution. The deduction must be periodically renewed by an act of Congress, and taxpayers should confirm it is available for 2018 before claiming it.

Other Adjustments to Income

Q Can I take a deduction for an Archer MSA?

A An Archer MSA is a medical savings account set up to pay the qualified medical expenses of you, your spouse and dependents. The contributions you make to an Archer MSA are deductible, subject to certain limitations. The deduction is taken by writing "MSA" and the deduction amount on the dotted line next to Line 36 of Form 1040, Schedule 1, Additional Income and Adjustments to Income.

Q Can I take a deduction for jury duty pay?

A If jury duty pay must be given to your employer because the employer pays your salary while you are on jury duty, you can deduct that amount on Form 1040, Schedule 1, Additional Income and Adjustments to Income, Line 36, by entering the amount on Line 36 and entering "Jury Pay" and the amount on the dotted line next to Line 36.

Q Can supplemental unemployment benefits be deducted?

A Supplemental unemployment benefits are unemployment benefits received from an employer-financed fund. These benefits are generally taxable as wages in the year received. If you are required to repay supplemental unemployment benefits in a later year in order to qualify for trade readjustment allowances under the Trade Act of 1974, you can deduct the amount of the repayment by writing "Sub-Pay TRA" and the amount of the deduction on the dotted line next to Line 36 of Form 1040, Schedule 1, Additional Income and Adjustments to Income.

Q Can I deduct attorney fees?

A You can deduct attorney fees and court costs paid to recover a judgment or settlement for the following types of unlawful discrimination claims by writing "UDC" and the amount of the deduction on the dotted line next to Line 36 of Form 1040, Schedule 1, Additional Income and Adjustments to Income:

1. a claim of unlawful discrimination under various provisions of federal, state and local law;
2. a claim against the U.S. government; or
3. a claim under Section 1862(b)(3)(A) of the Social Security Act.

You can deduct attorney fees and court costs paid in connection with an award received from the IRS for information that substantially contributes to the detection of tax law violations by writing "WBF" and the amount of the deduction on the dotted line next to Line 36 of Form 1040, Schedule 1, Additional Income and Adjustments to Income.

Deductions—Form 1040

Standard Deductions and Itemized Deductions

Q What are the basic standard deduction amounts for 2018?

A For 2018, the basic standard deduction amounts based on filing status are as follows:

1. Single: $12,000;
2. Married filing joint return/Qualifying widow(er) with dependent child: $24,000;
3. Married filing separate return: $12,000; and
4. Head of household: $18,000.

Q When should I claim itemized deductions instead of the standard deduction?

A You generally benefit from claiming itemized deductions if the total allowable itemized deductions for the year exceed your standard deduction.

Q What is the qualified business income deduction?

A The qualified business income deduction is new for 2018. It allows sole proprietors, shareholders in an S corporation, and partners in a partnership to claim a deduction for up to 20 percent of domestic qualified income from that sole proprietorship, S corporation or a partnership. The deduction has many rules relating to what is domestic income, what is qualified income, and the kinds of businesses that are allowed. The deduction does not have to be itemized, and it can be taken in addition to a standard deduction. It is claimed on Form 1040, U.S. Individual Income Tax Return, Line 9.

Itemized Deductions—Schedule A (Form 1040)

Medical and Dental Expenses

Q What are the general rules for deducting medical expenses?

A Expenses paid during the tax year for the medical care of the you, your spouse, and dependents generally are deductible on Lines 1 through 4 of Schedule A (Form 1040), Itemized Deductions. However, medical expenses are not deductible to the extent you are reimbursed for them by insurance or otherwise. Moreover, medical expenses are deductible only to the extent that they exceed 7.5 percent of your adjusted gross income (AGI).

Q What expenses are generally deductible as medical expenses?

A Medical expenses are amounts paid for the diagnosis, cure, mitigation, treatment, or prevention of disease, or for the purpose of affecting any structure or function of the body. Medical expenses include the cost of any service that facilitates the diagnosis of a physical or mental defect or illness and, thus, serves to prevent or alleviate such a defect or illness. However, medical expenses do not include expenses merely beneficial to general health, such as vacation expenses. Thus, medical expenses include the costs of medicine and drugs, the costs of surgery or treatments affecting a portion of the body, the costs of diagnostic services and devices, the costs of medical care at a hospital or other institution (including a retirement home) and the costs of nursing services. In some cases, capital expenses may also be deductible as medical expenses.

Medical expenses also include the costs of transportation primarily for and essential to medical care, the costs for qualified long-term care services or for any qualified long-term care insurance contract, and the costs of insurance covering medical care. The costs of dental care are also treated as medical expenses. Thus, fees paid to a dentist for x-rays, fillings, braces, extractions and dentures are deductible as medical expenses. However, the costs of teeth whitening generally are not deductible.

Deductible Taxes

Q What state and local income taxes are deductible?

A State and local income taxes that are generally deductible include:

1. State and local income taxes withheld from your compensation or other income during the current tax year. Such withheld taxes are reported to you on Form W-2 (Boxes 17 and 19), Form W-2G (Boxes 15 and 17), Form 1099-MISC (Box 16), Form 1099-R (Boxes 12 and 15), or Form 1099-G (Box 11).
2. State and local income taxes paid during the current tax year with respect to a prior year tax liability. Note that state and local income taxes generally are deductible only in the year in which they are actually paid.
3. Estimated state and local income taxes paid during the current tax year. An overpayment of prior year state and local income taxes that is credited to the current year is treated as an estimated tax payment for the current year.

The total amount of state and local taxes that can be deducted in 2018 is limited to $10,000.

Q What real estate taxes are deductible?

A Deductible real estate taxes are taxes that are:

1. based on the assessed value of property;
2. uniformly assessed against all real property under the jurisdiction of the tax authority; and
3. levied for the general public welfare.

Taxes are considered to be levied for the general public welfare only if the proceeds are used for general community or governmental purposes.

The total amount of state and local taxes that can be deducted in 2018 is limited to $10,000.

Q Are prepaid 2018 property taxes paid in 2017 deductible in 2018?

A No. Any property taxes paid at the end of 2017 that were attributable to 2018 but paid on a bill issued by a state or local authority before the end of 2017 should have been claimed on a 2017 tax return.

Deductible Interest

Q What are the general rules on deducting interest?

A Personal interest is not deductible. For this purpose, personal interest includes any interest that does not fall into one of the following six categories:

1. **Qualified residence interest.** This is interest allocable to debt used on a qualified residence.
2. **Investment interest.** This is interest allocable to debt used for investment.
3. **Interest on qualified education loans.** This is interest allocable to debt used for education.
4. **Passive activity interest.** This is interest allocable to debt used in a passive activity. Such interest is taken into account in determining the income or loss from the passive activity.
5. **Business interest.** This is interest allocable to debt used in a trade or business (other than interest allocable to debt used in the business of performing services as an employee, which is personal interest).
6. **Interest on deferred estate tax.** This is interest due to an election by an executor of an estate to defer payment of estate tax involving certain closely held businesses.

Q What are the general rules on deducting home mortgage interest?

A You may generally deduct interest paid during the tax year on a home mortgage. Such mortgage interest is deductible if:

1. the interest is paid with respect to a qualified residence in which you have an ownership interest;

2. the interest is be paid on a valid debt for which you are legally liable; and
3. the debt is secured by the qualified residence.

Deductible mortgage interest is known as qualified residence interest. Points and mortgage insurance premiums are also treated as qualified residence interest for purposes of these rules.

Q Are there limits on the home mortgage interest deduction?

A A deduction for home mortgage interest on a debt incurred to acquire a home after December 15, 2017, is limited to debt up to $750,000 ($375,000 for married taxpayers filing separately. The deduction is not available for any home equity debt incurred after 2017. For debts incurred on or before December 15, 2017, the limitation is $1,000,000 ($500,000 for married taxpayers filing separately). The deduction is available for home equity indebtedness incurred prior to 2018.

Charitable Contributions

Q What are the general rules on deducting charitable contributions?

A You can take an itemized deduction for charitable contributions on Lines 11 through 13 of Schedule A (Form 1040), Itemized Deductions. A charitable contribution is a voluntary donation or gift of money or property made to, or for the use of, a qualified charitable organization. As a general rule, you can deduct the amount of any money contributed or the fair market value of any property contributed in the year the contribution is made. However, there are certain limitations that may apply to the amount of contributions that may be deducted.

The limitations are generally based on the type of organization to which the contribution is made, the type of property that is contributed, and your adjusted gross income (AGI). If the amount of a contribution is limited, the unused portion may be carried over and deducted in subsequent years.

Certain substantiation requirements must be satisfied with respect to charitable contribution deductions. These requirements generally depend on the type and amount of the contribution.

Q **What are the limitations on deducting charitable contributions?**

A For 2018, charitable contributions are limited to 60 percent, 30 percent, or 20 percent of your contribution base, defined as adjusted gross income (AGI) without regard to net operating loss carrybacks. The limitations are determined by the charity classification and the type of contribution made. In addition, capital gain property may be subject to limits on the value of the contribution. Contributions made in excess of the limitation can be carried over for five years.

Casualty and Theft Losses

Q **Can I deduct a casualty loss?**

A A casualty loss is a loss resulting from damage to, or destruction of, property except that for nonbusiness property, the deduction is limited to losses arising from fire, storm, shipwreck, or other casualty, or from theft. Casualty losses that are not compensated for by insurance or otherwise are generally deductible. However, for 2018, a casualty loss can only be claimed for losses attributable to federally declared disasters.

Q **What limitations apply to the deduction of a casualty or theft loss?**

A For 2018, the deduction for casualty and theft losses of personal use property and employee property is subject to limitation. A loss of personal use property is subject to a $100 floor and the 10-percent AGI limitation.

Q **How is the amount of a casualty or theft loss figured?**

A The amount of a casualty or theft loss is calculated as the lesser of:

1. the decrease in the fair market value of the property as a result of the casualty or theft (i.e., the fair market value of the property immediately before the casualty or theft reduced by the fair market value of the property immediately after the casualty or theft); or
2. the adjusted basis of the property.

Other Itemized Deductions

Q What are some other itemized deductions?

A For 2018, other itemized deductions allowed on Line 16 of Schedule A of Form 1040 include the following expenses and losses:

1. gambling losses;
2. casualty and theft losses of income-producing property;
3. certain losses reported to you by an electing large partnership;
4. the federal estate tax paid on income in respect of a decedent;
5. the amortizable premium on certain taxable bonds;
6. ordinary losses attributable to a contingent payment debt instrument or an inflation-indexed debt instrument;
7. repayments of more than $3,000 under a claim of right;
8. the unrecovered investment in an annuity of a deceased taxpayer; and
9. the impairment-related work expenses of persons with disabilities (Instructions for Schedule A).

These are the only expenses and losses that may be deducted on Line 16 of Schedule A.

Q How are the gambling losses of recreational gamblers treated for tax purposes?

A The gambling losses of recreational gamblers are deductible as a miscellaneous itemized deduction on Line 16 of Schedule A. However, such gambling losses are only deductible to the extent of gambling winnings. For 2018, losses can include any expenses related to gambling that would otherwise be deductible as a business expense. Gambling winnings must be reported as income on Line 21 of Form 1040, Schedule 1, Additional Income and Adjustments to Income.

Tax—Form 1040

Regular Tax

Q Who must use the Foreign Earned Income Tax Worksheet to calculate regular tax?

A If you claimed the foreign income exclusion or the foreign housing exclusion on Form 2555, Foreign Earned Income, or Form 2555-EZ, Foreign Earned Income Exclusion, you must use the Foreign Earned Income Tax Worksheet to calculate the regular tax.

Q Who should use the Qualified Dividends and Capital Gain Tax Worksheet to calculate regular tax?

A You generally must use the Qualified Dividends and Capital Gain Tax Worksheet to calculate the regular tax if the Schedule D Tax Worksheet does not apply to you and:

1. you reported qualified dividends on Line 3a of Form 1040;
2. you ae not required to file Schedule D, and reported capital gain distributions on Line 13 of Form 1040, Schedule 1; or
3. you are required to file Schedule D, and Lines 15 and 16 of Schedule D are both more than zero.

Q Who is a child for purposes of the kiddie tax?

A For purposes of the kiddie tax, a "child" is defined to include:

1. any individual who is under age 18 at the end of the year;
2. any individual who is age 18 at the end of the year and whose earned income does not provide more than half of his or her support for the year; and
3. a student who is age 19 through 23 (i.e., under age 24) at the end of the year and whose earned income does not provide more than half of his or her support for the year.

For purposes of this rule, a student is any individual who is a full-time student at an educational organization or pursuing a full-time course of institutional farm training for five months during the year. A student's support for the year does not include amounts received as scholarships for study at an educational organization.

Q Who does the kiddie tax apply to?

A The kiddie tax applies to a child for 2018 if:

1. a child has investment income of more than $2,100;
2. the child is required to file an income tax return, but does not file a joint return; and
3. at least one of the child's parents is alive at the end of the year.

However, the kiddie tax does not apply if a parent elects to report the child's income by filing Form 8814.

Tax—Schedule 2 (Form 1040)

Alternative Minimum Tax

Q Why is there an alternative minimum tax (AMT)?

A Because federal tax law gives special treatment to some types of income and allows special deductions and credits for some types of expenses, some taxpayers with substantial economic income can significantly reduce their regular tax. The purpose of the AMT is to ensure that these taxpayers pay a minimum amount of tax on their economic income.

Q What are the 2018 AMT exemption amounts?

A For 2018, the exemption amounts are $70,300 for single taxpayers and head of household; $109,400 for married filing jointly and surviving spouse; and $54,700 for married filing separately. There are also special exemption amounts for certain minor children.

For 2018, the AMTI exemption amount for a child subject to the kiddie tax is the lesser of:
1. $70,300; or
2. the sum of the child's earned income plus $7,600.

Q What is the 2018 AMT tax rate?

A There is a two-tiered, graduated rate schedule for the AMT. For 2018, a 26-percent tax rate applies to the first $191,100 of alternative minimum taxable income (AMTI) in excess of the applicable AMT exemption amount. A 28-percent tax rate applies to AMTI more than $191,100 ($95,550 for married filing separately).

Tax Credits—Form 1040

Child Tax Credit

Q What is the maximum amount of the child tax credit that may generally be claimed and who may claim it?

A The child tax credit may be claimed by taxpayers who have one or more qualifying children. For 2018, the maximum amount that can be claimed for the child tax credit is $2,000 for each qualifying child. However, the child tax credit is subject to an income limitation. Additionally, a $500 credit ("family credit") may be claimed for certain dependents who are not qualifying children. The credit is reduced or eliminated for joint filers with modified adjusted gross income in excess of $400,000 ($200,000 all other filers).

Q For purposes of the child tax credit, who is a qualifying child?

A For purposes of the child tax credit, a qualifying child is a child who:

1. is you son, daughter, stepchild, adopted child, foster child, brother, sister, stepbrother, stepsister, or a descendent of any of them (relationship test);
2. was under age 17 at the end of 2018 (age test);
3. lived with you for more than half of the year (residency test);
4. did not provide over half of his or her own support for the year (support test);
5. was a U.S. citizen, U.S. national, or U.S. resident (citizenship test); and
6. does not file a joint return for the year, unless the return is made solely to claim a refund.

Q For purposes of the $500 family credit, who is a qualifying relative?

A A qualifying relative is a dependent who is not a qualifying child. A dependent for this purpose is an individual:

1. who bears a specific relationship (child, grandchild, sibling, step-sibling, parent, grandparent, niece, nephew, aunt, uncle, in-law, or any person who shares your home and is a member of your household) to you;
2. whose gross income for the calendar year in which your tax year begins is less than the exemption amount ($4,150 for 2018);
3. who receives over one-half of his or her support from the taxpayer for the calendar year in which the tax year begins; and
4. who is not a qualifying child of you or any other taxpayer for any tax year beginning in the calendar year in which your tax year begins.

Q Can I claim the child tax credit if I do not owe taxes?

A A portion of the child tax credit can be claimed when the amount of the credit due is more than taxes owed. This is known as a refundable credit, or in this case, the additional child tax credit. The amount of the additional child tax credit is limited to $1,400 per child for 2018.

Nonrefundable Tax Credits— Schedule 3 (Form 1040)

Foreign Tax Credit

Q What foreign taxes qualify for the foreign tax credit?

A Generally, the following four tests must be met for any foreign tax to qualify for the credit:

1. the tax must be imposed on the taxpayer;
2. you must have paid or accrued the tax;
3. the tax must be the legal and actual foreign tax liability; and
4. the tax must be an income, war profits, or excess profits tax (or a tax in lieu of those taxes).

Q Can I take a foreign tax credit for taxes for which a refund is available?

A No foreign tax credit is allowed for taxes not legally owed. Thus, for example, portfolio investors may not be entitled to the full amount of foreign tax shown on a payee statement (e.g., Form 1099-DIV) if the investor is entitled to a refund of foreign tax withheld because of a reduced treaty withholding rate. The investor is only entitled to a foreign tax credit for the reduced amount, whether or not the investor files a refund claim with the foreign tax authorities.

Q Can a cash method taxpayer take a foreign tax credit in the year the taxes accrue?

A Even taxpayers using the cash method of accounting can choose to take a credit for foreign taxes in the year they accrue. You make that choice by checking a box on Form 1116. Once that choice is made, however, you must follow it in all later years and take a credit for foreign taxes in the year they accrue. In addition, the choice to take the credit when foreign taxes accrue applies to all foreign taxes qualified for the credit. You cannot take a credit for some foreign taxes when paid and take a credit for others when accrued.

Business Tax Credits

Q How much is the credit for small employer pension plan startup costs?

A The amount of the credit is limited to $500 for the first credit year and for each of the two tax years immediately following the first credit year. Thus, it is available only for three years. The first credit year is the tax year that includes the date that the plan to which the costs relate becomes effective but, at the election of the employer, the first credit year may be the year preceding the year the plan becomes effective. You make this election by claiming the credit on your return for the year preceding the year in which the plan becomes effective.

Q What is the disabled tax credit and how much is it?

A The disabled access credit is a credit for certain expenses paid or incurred by a small business to make the business accessible to disabled persons. Specifically, an eligible small business may claim a credit for 50 percent of its eligible access expenditures that exceed $250 in a tax year, but do not exceed $10,250.

Other Taxes—Schedule 4 (Form 1040)

Self-Employment Tax

Q Who is subject to self-employment (SE) tax?

A A U.S. citizen or resident alien is subject to the SE tax for a tax year if the individual had:

1. net earnings from self-employment (other than church employee income) of $400 or more for the year; or
2. church employee income of $108.28 or more for the year.

Q Which taxpayers must always use the Long Schedule SE (Section B)?

A The following taxpayers must always use the Long Schedule SE (Section B):

1. individuals who use the nonfarm optional method or the farm optional method to figure net earnings from self employment;
2. ministers, members of religious orders, or Christian Science practitioners who received IRS approval not to be taxed on their ministerial earnings, but who owe self-employment tax on nonministerial earnings;
3. individuals who received church employee income reported on Form W-2 of $108.28 or more;
4. individuals whose total of their wages and tips subject to Social Security tax plus their net earnings from self employment was more than the Social Security wage base for the year;
5. individuals who received tips subject to Social Security or Medicare tax but who not report those tips to their employers; and
6. individuals who reported any wages on Form 8919, Uncollected Social Security and Medicare Tax on Wages.

Tax Payments

Q Who is required to file Form 1040, Schedule H, for household employees?

A A Schedule H must be filed if any of the following conditions are met:

1. You paid any one household employee $2,100 or more in wages during 2018, the household employee does not include your spouse, child under age 21, parent (unless there was a child under 18 or a disabled child with a physical or mental condition requiring personal adult care for at least four continuous weeks in the home during the calendar year), and you are divorced or not remarried, a widow, or widower, or married to and living with a person whose physical or mental condition prevented him or her from caring for the child described above during at least four continuous weeks during the calendar year; or
2. You withheld federal income tax for any household employee during 2018.

Filing and Paying—Form 1040

Filing

Q When is Form 1040 due?

A Individual income tax returns for U.S. citizens and resident aliens are due on or before the 15th day of the fourth month following the close of the tax year.

If a tax return's due date is a Saturday, Sunday, or legal holiday, the due date is the next day that is not a Saturday, Sunday, or legal holiday. A legal holiday is a legal holiday in the District of Columbia (e.g., April 16, Emancipation Day, is a legal holiday in the District of Columbia). If the return is to be filed in an IRS office outside the District of Columbia, the term "legal holiday" includes any statewide legal holiday for the state in which the return is to be filed. For example, for taxpayers filing returns in Massachusetts or Maine, Patriots' Day, which generally falls in mid-April, is a legal holiday, because it is a statewide holiday in those states.

That date is April 15, 2019, for calendar-year taxpayers. However, for taxpayers in Massachusetts or Maine, April 15, 2019, is Patriot's Day, and because Emancipation Day in the District of Columbia is April 16, 2019, Form 1040 is due April 17, 2019, for taxpayers in those states.

Q When is a decedent's tax return due?

A A decedent's final income tax return is due on the date that the return would have been due had the decedent lived. Generally, the personal representative must file the final income tax return of the decedent for the year of death and any returns not filed for preceding years. A surviving spouse, under certain circumstances, may have to file the returns for the decedent).

Estimated Tax Penalty

Q How can I avoid the underpayment of estimated tax penalty?

A No penalty is assessed for underpayment of estimated taxes when at least 100 percent of the tax shown on the prior year return is paid through estimated payments and/or withholding before the due date for the last estimated payment. The percentage increases to 110 percent for high-income filers with adjusted gross income in excess of $150,000 ($75,000 for married filing separate returns). This applies only if the prior year's tax return was for a full 12 months.

Appendix
Taxpayers Affected by the Tax Cuts and Jobs Act

¶10 Effect on Individuals, Generally

Individual income tax rates.—The individual income tax rates and bracket amounts are modified for tax years 2018 through 2025. The temporary tax rates are 10, 12, 22, 24, 32, 35, and 37 percent.

Alternative minimum tax (AMT).—The AMT exemption amounts are temporarily increased for individuals after 2017 and before 2026. Beginning in 2018, the exemption amounts are $109,400 for married individuals filing separately or surviving spouses, $70,300 for single or head of household filers, and $54,700 for married filing separately. The phaseout thresholds are also temporarily increased after 2017 to $1 million if married filing jointly or surviving spouse and $500,000 for all other individuals.

Individual health insurance mandate.—Effective for months beginning after December 31, 2018, the amount owed by any taxpayer under the individual health insurance mandate "shared responsibility payment" for lack of minimum essential health insurance for themselves and their dependents is zero.

Standard deduction.—The basic standard deduction amounts are increased to: $12,000 for single individuals and married individuals filing separately; $18,000 for heads of household; and $24,000 for married individuals filing jointly (including surviving spouses). The increased amounts, which are adjusted annually for inflation, are effective for tax years 2018 through 2025.

Personal and dependency exemptions.—The deduction for personal and dependency exemptions is temporarily repealed for tax years 2018 through 2025.

State and local tax deduction.—The itemized deduction by individuals for state, local, and foreign property taxes, and state and local income taxes and general sales taxes paid or accrued during the tax year is limited for tax years 2018 through 2025. An individual cannot deduct foreign real property taxes, but may still claim an itemized deduction of up to $10,000 ($5,000 for married taxpayer filing a separate return) for state and local property taxes, income taxes, and general sales taxes paid or accrued in the tax year.

Personal casualty and theft losses.—The itemized deduction for personal casualty and theft losses is limited to those attributable to a federally declared disaster.

Moving expenses.—The deduction for moving expenses is temporarily repealed for tax years 2018 through 2025. The exclusion for qualified moving expense reimbursements is suspended for tax years 2018 through 2025.

¶12 Effect on Homeowners

State and local tax deduction.—The itemized deduction of individuals for state, local, and foreign property taxes, and state and local income taxes and general sales taxes paid or accrued during the tax year is limited for tax years 2018 through 2025. An individual cannot deduct foreign real property taxes, but may still claim an itemized deduction of up to $10,000 ($5,000 for married taxpayer filing a separate return) for state and local property taxes, income taxes, and general sales taxes paid or accrued in the tax year.

Home mortgage interest.—The itemized deduction for home mortgage interest is subject to new limitations for tax years 2018 through 2025. A taxpayer is limited to claiming the home mortgage interest deduction only for interest paid or accrued on acquisition debt during those years; the deduction of interest on home equity debt is suspended. The maximum amount that may be treated as acquisition debt is also reduced to $750,000 ($375,000 if married filing separately) for any acquisition debt incurred after December 15, 2017.

Personal casualty and theft losses.—The itemized deduction for personal casualty and theft losses is limited to those attributable to a federally declared disaster.

Mortgage information on Form 1098.—Form 1098 is required to include the amount of the outstanding mortgage, the address of the property, and the loan origination date.

¶14 Effect on High-Income Taxpayers

Alternative minimum tax (AMT).—The AMT exemption amounts are temporarily increased for individuals after 2017 and before 2026. Beginning in 2018, the exemption amounts are $109,400 for married individuals filing separately or surviving spouses, $70,300 for single or head of household filers, and $54,700 for married filing separately. The phaseout thresholds are also temporarily increased after 2017 to $1 million if married filing jointly or surviving spouse and $500,000 for all other individuals.

Itemized deduction.—The overall limitation on itemized deductions is suspended, applicable to tax years beginning after 2017 and before 2026.

Employee compensation.—For purposes of the limitation on the deduction for employee compensation paid by publicly held corporations, the definition of covered employee is expanded to include both the principal executive officer and the principal financial officer, as well as the other three most highly compensated employees. Employees who are covered employees after December 31, 2016, remain as covered employees for all future tax years.

The exclusions from the limitation for commission-based and performance based compensation have been repealed.

Executive compensation.—A new excise tax has been established, payable by exempt organizations on remuneration in excess of $1 million and any excess parachute payments made to certain highly-compensated current and former employees in the tax year.

¶15 Effect on Seniors

Estate, gift, and generation-skipping transfer tax.—The basic exclusion amount for purposes of federal estate and gift taxes and the exemption amount for purposes of the generation-skipping transfer (GST) tax is doubled from $5 million to $10 million, before adjustment for inflation, for the estates of decedents dying and gifts and generation-skipping transfers made after 2017 and before 2026.

Medical expenses.—The adjusted gross income (AGI) threshold to claim itemized deduction for unreimbursed expenses paid for the medical care of the taxpayer or the taxpayer's spouse or dependents is temporarily reduced to 7.5 percent of AGI.

¶17 Effect on Investors

Rollover of capital gain.—The election to defer recognition of capital gain realized on the sale of publicly traded securities if the taxpayer used the sale proceeds to purchase common stock or a partnership interest in a specialized small business investment company (SSBIC) is repealed.

¶18 Effect on Disabled Persons

ABLE accounts.—Individuals are allowed to roll over amounts from qualified tuition plans (also known as section 529 plans) to an ABLE account if the ABLE account is owned by the same designated beneficiary of the 529 plan or a member of the designated beneficiary's family before January 1, 2026. Under certain circumstances, the contribution limitation to ABLE accounts is increased for contributions made by the designated beneficiary before January 1, 2026.

¶19 Effect on Bond Investors

Advanced refunding bonds.—Interest paid on advance refunding bonds issued after 2017 is not excludable from gross income as interest paid on state and local government bonds.

Tax credit bonds.—New tax credit bonds cannot be issued after December 31, 2017.

¶21 Effect on Parents

Personal and dependency exemptions.—The deduction for personal and dependency exemptions is temporarily repealed for tax years 2018 through 2025.

   Child tax credit.—The child tax credit is temporarily expanded after 2017 by increasing the credit amount for each qualifying child to $2,000, increasing the phaseout threshold to $400,000 if married filing jointly ($200,000 for other taxpayers), and providing a $500 nonrefundable credit for each dependent who is not a qualifying child. The refundable portion of the credit (additional child tax credit) is limited to $1,400 per qualifying child, but is indexed for inflation and the earned income threshold is reduced to $2,500. A taxpayer must include a qualifying child's Social Security number on his or her return to receive the nonrefundable or refundable portion of the credit with respect to the child.

   Qualified tuition programs.—Section 529 qualified tuition plans are modified to allow the plans to distribute no more than $10,000 in tuition expenses incurred during the tax year for designated beneficiaries enrolled at a public, private, or religious elementary or secondary school.

   ABLE accounts.—Individuals are allowed to roll over amounts from qualified tuition plans (also known as section 529 plans) to an ABLE account if the ABLE account is owned by the same designated beneficiary of the 529 plan or a member of the designated beneficiary's family before January 1, 2026. Under certain circumstances, the contribution limitation to ABLE accounts is increased for contributions made by the designated beneficiary before January 1, 2026.

¶23 Effect on Students

Student loans.—Eligibility to exclude discharge of student loan debt from gross income is temporarily expanded to include discharges of eligible student loans before 2026 due to the student's death or total and permanent disability.

   Qualified tuition programs.—Section 529 qualified tuition plans are modified to allow the plans to distribute no more than $10,000 in tuition expenses incurred during the tax year for designated beneficiaries enrolled at a public, private, or religious elementary or secondary school.

¶24 Effect on Military Personnel

Hazardous duty area.—The Sinai Peninsula of Egypt is a qualified hazardous duty area for the applicable period and is treated the same as a combat zone for purposes of certain tax benefits for members of the U.S. Armed Forces. The applicable period is generally the portion of the first tax year beginning after June 9, 2015, and any subsequent tax year beginning before January 1, 2026.

Moving expenses.—The deduction for moving expenses is temporarily repealed for tax years 2018 through 2025. The exclusion for qualified moving expense reimbursements is suspended for tax years 2018 through 2025. However, the special rules for a member of the Armed Forces to deduct moving expenses and exclude in-kind moving expenses, and reimbursements or allowances, continues to apply during these tax years.

¶25 Effect on Employees

Miscellaneous itemized deductions.—The deductibility of miscellaneous itemized deductions is temporarily repealed for tax years 2018 through 2025.

Employee stock options.—Employees who are granted stock options are able to elect to defer recognition of income for up to five years. The election is not available to certain executives, highly compensated officers, and "one-percent owners" of the corporation. The corporation must maintain a written plan under which at least 80 percent of all employees providing services to the corporation are granted stock options with the same rights and privileges.

Moving expenses.—The exclusion for qualified moving expense reimbursements is suspended for tax years 2018 through 2025.

Bicycle commuting expenses.—After December 31, 2017, and before January 1, 2026, taxpayers are not permitted to exclude any amount from their income for qualified bicycle commuting reimbursements.

¶26 Effect on Inventors

Self-created property.—A patent, invention, model or design (patented or not), or secret formula or process is excluded the definition of a capital asset for dispositions after December 31, 2017, if it is held by the taxpayer who created the property or a taxpayer with a substituted or transferred basis from the taxpayer who created the property.

¶27 Effect on Professional Gamblers

Gambling losses.—The rule that a deduction for wagering losses is limited to the amount of wagering winnings, applies not only to the actual costs of wagers, but to other expenses incurred by the individual in connection with that individual's gambling activities.

¶30 Effect on Public Safety Officers and Their Survivors

Length of service award exclusion for bona fide public safety volunteers.—The dollar limit on the length of service award exclusion from Code Sec. 457 for bona fide public safety volunteers is doubled from $3,000 to $6,000 effective for tax years beginning after December 31, 2017.

¶32 Effect on Charitable Donors

Charitable contribution deductions.—The percentage limitation on the charitable deduction contribution base is increased to 60 percent of an individual's adjusted gross income for cash donations to public charities in 2018 through 2025. The deduction for amounts paid for college athletic seating rights is repealed. The exception to contemporaneous written acknowledgment requirement for contributions of $250 or more is repealed.

Charitable contribution deduction for electing small business trust.—The charitable contribution deduction of an ESBT is generally to be determined by the rules applicable to individuals, not to the rules generally applicable to trusts. This change applies to tax years beginning after December 31, 2017.

¶33 Effect on International Business

Treatment of sale or exchange of partnership interests by foreign persons.—Gain or loss from the sale or exchange of a partnership interest is effectively connected with a U.S. trade or business to the extent that the transferor would have had effectively connected gain or loss had the partnership sold all of its assets at fair market value as of the disposition date. The transferee of a partnership interest must withhold 10 percent of the amount realized on the sale or exchange unless the transferor certifies that it is not a nonresident alien or foreign corporation.

¶36 Effect on Retirement Plan Participants

Recharacterization of IRA contributions.—The special rule that allows a contribution to one type of an IRA to be recharacterized as a contribution to the other type of IRA will no longer apply to a conversion contribution to a Roth IRA after 2017. Recharacterization is still permitted with respect to other contributions. For example, an individual may make a contribution for a year to a Roth IRA and, before the due date for the individual's income tax return for that year, recharacterize it as a contribution to a traditional IRA.

Rollovers of plan loan offset amounts.—For plan loan offset amounts that are treated as distributed after 2017, a participant whose plan terminates or who is severed from employment while having a plan loan outstanding will have until the due date for filing their tax return for that year to contribute the loan balance to an IRA in order to avoid the loan being taxed as a distribution IRA.

Qualified 2016 disaster distributions from retirement plans.—The 10 percent additional tax under Code Sec. 72(t) is waived for any qualified 2016 disaster distribution. Eligible individuals who take such distributions can spread their taxable income over three years, and have three years to repay the amount.

¶38 Effect on Businesses Generally

Section 179 expensing.—The section 179 dollar limitation is increased to $1 million and the investment limitation is increased to $2.5 million for tax years beginning after 2017. The definition of qualified real property eligible for expensing is redefined to include improvements to the interior of any nonresidential real property ("qualified improvement property"), as well as roofs, heating, ventilation, and air-conditioning property, fire protection and alarm systems, and security systems installed on such property. The exclusion from expensing for property used in connecting with lodging facilities, such as residential rental property, is eliminated. The $25,000 section 179 expensing limit on certain heavy vehicles is inflation-adjusted after 2018.

Bonus depreciation-generally—The bonus depreciation rate is increased to 100 percent for property acquired and placed in service after September 27, 2017 and before January 1, 2023. The rate phases down thereafter. Used property and films, television shows, and theatrical productions are eligible for bonus depreciation. Property used by rate-regulated utilities and property of certain motor vehicle, boat, and farm machinery retail and lease businesses that use floor financing indebtedness is excluded from bonus depreciation.

Depreciation of luxury cars.—The annual limits on depreciation deductions for "luxury cars" are almost quadrupled for property placed in service after 2017. The IRS will need to issue a safe harbor in order to allow taxpayers to claim depreciation after the first year a vehicle is placed in service if the 100 percent bonus depreciation deduction is claimed.

Computers as listed property.—Computers and related peripheral equipment are no longer "listed property" subject to strict substantiation and depreciation requirements, effective for property placed in service after December 31, 2017.

Recovery periods for MACRS real property.—Assuming a technical correction is enacted, qualified improvement property is assigned a 15-year recovery period as intended by Congress. The property classes for 15-year leasehold improvement property, retail improvement property, and restaurant property are eliminated. The MACRS alternative depreciation system (ADS) must be used by an electing real property trade or business to depreciate residential rental property, nonresidential real property, and qualified improvement property.

Limitation on deduction of business interest.—The deduction of business interest is limited for any tax year beginning after 2017 to the sum of the taxpayer's business interest income, floor plan financing, and 30 percent of adjusted taxable income. The limitation generally applies to all taxpayers, but does not apply for small businesses with average gross receipts of $25 million or less (adjusted for inflation). Any disallowed interest generally may be carried forward indefinitely. In the case of a partnership or S corporation, the deduction limitation applies at the entity level, except that disallowed interest of the entity is allocated to each partner or shareholder as excess business interest.

Net operating losses.—Net operating losses (NOLs) may no longer be carried back but may be carried forward indefinitely. However, the five-year carryback period for farming losses is reduced to two years and a two-year carryback and 20-year carryforward period is retained for insurance companies other than life insurance companies. A net operating loss may only reduce 80 percent of taxable income in a carryback or carryforward tax year. The taxable income limitation does not apply to non-life insurance companies.

Excess business losses for noncorporate taxpayers.—Excess business losses of noncorporate taxpayers are not allowed for tax years beginning in 2018 through 2025. Any disallowed excess business loss is treated as a net operating loss (NOL) carryover to the following tax year. However, the passive activity loss rules apply before application of the excess business loss rules.

Research and experimental expenditures.—Research and experimental expenditures paid or accrued after 2021 generally must be amortized ratably over five years. Any amount paid or incurred in connection with the development of any software is treated as a research or experimental expenditure for this purposes of this amortization provision. A 15-year amortization period applies to research or experimental expenditures attributable to foreign research.

Domestic production activities deduction.—The domestic production activities deduction (DPAD) under Code Sec. 199 is repealed for tax years beginning after 2017.

Employer's deduction for entertainment, commuting benefits, and meals.—Business expense deductions are eliminated for some entertainment costs and commuting benefits after 2017 and for some employer-provided meal expenses after 2025.

Non-tangible personal property as employee achievement awards.—For purposes of employee achievement awards, employers are prohibited from deducting awards that are given in cash, cash equivalents, gift cards, gift coupons, gift certificates, vacations, meals, lodging, tickets to theater or sporting events, stocks, bonds, other securities or similar items.

Employee compensation.—For purposes of the limitation on the deduction for employee compensation paid by publicly held corporations, the definition of covered employee is expanded to include both the principal executive officer and the principal financial officer, as well as the other three most highly compensated employees. Employees who are covered employees after December 31, 2016, remain as covered employees for all future tax years. The exclusions from the limitation for commission-based and performance based compensation have been repealed.

Fines and penalties.—Businesses may not deduct fines and penalties incurred due to the violation of a law (or the investigation of a violation) if a government (or similar entity) is a complainant or investigator. Exceptions to this rule are available in certain cases where the payment was compensation for damages, compliance with the law, paid to satisfy a court order where the government is not a party, or paid for taxes due.

Local lobbying expenses.—The deduction for local lobbying expenses by a taxpayer as an ordinary and necessary business is repealed for expenses paid after December 22, 2017.

Paid family and medical leave.—Eligible employers are entitled to claim a credit for paid family and medical leave equal to 12.5 percent of wages paid to qualifying employees during any period in which such employees are on family and medical leave (FML) provided that the rate of payment is 50 percent of the wages normally paid to the employee. The credit is part of the general business credit and only available for wages paid in tax years beginning after December 31, 2017, and before January 1, 2020.

¶39 Effect on Passthrough Entities

Qualified business income deduction (passthrough deduction).—Noncorporate taxpayers may deduct up to 20 percent of domestic qualified business income from a partnership, S corporation, or sole proprietorship. A similar deduction is allowed for specified agricultural or horticultural cooperatives. A limitation based on wages paid, or on wages paid plus a capital element, is phased in for taxpayers with taxable income above a threshold amount. The deduction is not allowed for certain service trades or businesses, but this disallowance is phased in for lower income taxpayers. The deduction applies to tax years 2018 through 2025.

Basis limitation on partner losses.—The basis limitation on partner losses applies to a partner's distributive share of charitable contributions and foreign taxes.

Substantial built-in loss upon transfer of partnership interest.—The Code Sec. 743 definition of a "substantial built-in loss" is modified so that a substantial built-in loss also exists if the transferee would be allocated a net loss in excess of $250,000 upon a hypothetical disposition at fair market value by the partnership of all partnership assets immediately after the transfer of the partnership interest.

Treatment of sale or exchange of partnership interests by foreign persons.—Gain or loss from the sale or exchange of a partnership interest is effectively connected with a U.S. trade or business to the extent that the transferor would have had effectively connected gain or loss had the partnership sold all of its assets at fair market value as of the disposition date. The transferee of a partnership interest must withhold 10 percent of the amount realized on the sale or exchange unless the transferor certifies that it is not a nonresident alien or foreign corporation.

Technical termination of partnerships.—The rule providing for technical termination of partnerships is repealed for partnership tax years beginning after December 31, 2017.

¶41 Effect on Foreign Entities and Activities

Foreign-source portion of dividends.—Effective generally for distributions after December 31, 2017, a 100-percent participation exemption deduction is allowed for the foreign-source portion of dividends received from specified 10-percent owned foreign corporations by U.S. corporate shareholders, subject to a one-year holding period (a participation dividends-received deduction

(DRD)). No foreign tax credit or deduction is allowed for any taxes paid or accrued with respect to a dividend that qualifies for the deduction. The participation DRD is not available for hybrid dividends received from CFCs.

Specified 10-percent owned foreign corporations.—Amounts received by a domestic corporation upon the sale or exchange of stock in a foreign corporation held for at least one year that are treated as Section 1248 dividends are also treated as dividends for purposes of the participation dividends-received deduction (DRD).

Deferred foreign income upon transition to participation exemption system of taxation.—A transition tax is generally imposed on accumulated foreign earnings, without requiring an actual distribution, upon the transition to the new participation exemption system. Under the transition rule, for the last tax year beginning before January 1, 2018, any U.S. shareholder of any CFC or other foreign corporation (other than a PFIC that is not a CFC) that is at least 10-percent owned by a domestic corporation must include in income its pro rata share of the accumulated post-1986 foreign earnings of the corporation as of November 2, 2017, or December 31, 2017, whichever amount is greater (mandatory inclusion).

Recapture of overall domestic losses.—A taxpayer may elect to recapture pre-2018 unused overall domestic losses (ODLs) by recharacterizing up to 100 percent of the taxpayer's U.S. source taxable income as foreign source taxable income, from 2018 through 2027.

Foreign Tax Credit.—The Code Sec. 902 deemed-paid foreign tax credit is repealed and the Code Sec. 960 deemed-paid foreign tax credit is modified so that it is determined on a current year basis. A new foreign tax credit limitation basket is added for foreign branch income.

Cross-border inventory sales.—Income from cross-border sales of inventory is sourced on the basis of the production activities.

U.S. shareholders of controlled foreign corporations.—A current year inclusion of global intangible low-taxed income (GILTI) by a person who is a U.S. shareholder of a controlled foreign corporation (CFC). Domestic corporations are provided with reduced rates of U.S. tax on their foreign-derived intangible income (FDII) and global intangible low-taxed income (GILTI).

Foreign base company oil related income.—Foreign base company oil related income is eliminated as a category of foreign base company income and so is no longer subpart F income.

Withdrawal of qualified investments.—The subpart F inclusion for a CFC's previously excluded subpart F income withdrawn from foreign base company shipping operations is repealed. Also repealed is the subpart F inclusion for amounts withdrawn from qualified investment in less developed countries and decreases in export trade assets.

CFC stock attribution rules.—Stock ownership may be attributed downward from a foreign person to a related U.S. person for purposes of determining whether a U.S. person is a U.S. shareholder of a corporation, such that the foreign corporation is a CFC.

Definition of U.S. shareholder.—The definition of a U.S. shareholder is expanded to include a shareholder who owns 10 percent or more of a foreign corporation's stock by value. The definition of a U.S. shareholder now applies for purposes of Title 26.

Period of CFC status.—The requirement that a foreign corporation must be a CFC for an uninterrupted period of 30 days or more before a U.S. shareholder is required to include amounts in gross income under Subpart F is eliminated.

Base erosion and anti-abuse tax.—Applicable taxpayers are required to pay tax equal to the base erosion minimum tax amount for the tax year. The base erosion minimum tax amount is generally derived by comparing 10 percent (five percent for tax years beginning in calendar year 2018) of the taxpayer's modified taxable income (determined by disregarding certain deductions with respect to base erosion payments made to foreign related persons) to the taxpayer's regular tax liability (reduced for certain credit amounts). For tax years beginning after December 31, 2025, the 10-percent rate is increased to 12.5 percent and the taxpayer's regular tax liability is reduced by the aggregate amount of allowable credits. Applicable taxpayers include corporations (except RICs, REITs, or S corporations) with average annual gross receipts of at least $500 million over the past three tax years and a base erosion percentage of three percent (determined by dividing the aggregate deductions with respect to base erosion payments by the aggregate amount of allowed deductions with some exceptions). An 11-percent rate and two percent base erosion percentage apply to taxpayers that are members of an affiliated group that includes a bank or registered securities dealer. In addition, new reporting requirements will require the collection of information regarding a taxpayer's base erosion payments and the applicable penalty for failure to report is increased.

Income shifting through intangible property transfers.—The Code Sec. 936(h)(3)(B) definition of intangible property is modified to include goodwill, going concern value, and workforce in place as well as any other item the value of which is not attributable to tangible property or services of any individual. The new law also clarifies the authority of the Secretary of the Treasury to require the use of certain valuation methods in determining the value of intangible property in the context of Code Sec. 367(d) transfers and Code Sec. 482 intercompany pricing allocations.

Related party payments involving hybrid entities or hybrid transactions.—A deduction is not allowed for any disqualified related party amount paid or accrued in a hybrid transaction or by, or to, a hybrid entity.

Surrogate foreign corporation dividends.—Dividends received from surrogate foreign corporations are not eligible for lower tax rate treatment as qualified dividend income.

Insiders in expatriated corporations.—The excise tax rate on stock compensation received by insiders in an expatriated corporation increases from 15 percent to 20 percent.

Passive foreign investment company rules.—The rule for determining what is not considered passive income for a passive foreign investment company (PFIC) has been modified. The test for nonpassive income that is based on whether a corporation is predominantly engaged in an insurance business has been replaced with a test based on the amount of the corporation's insurance liabilities.

Interest expense.—The fair market value method for allocating and apportioning interest expense may no longer be used.

¶42 Effect on Small Businesses

Miscellaneous itemized deductions.—The deductibility of miscellaneous itemized deductions is temporarily repealed for tax years 2018 through 2025.

Methods of accounting.—The cash method of accounting and other simpler accounting methods have been made available to more taxpayers. Most taxpayers who meet a $25 million average annual gross receipts test will be able to use the cash method, will not be required to apply the inventory or uniform capitalization (UNICAP) rules, and will not be required to use the percentage of completion method for small construction contracts.

¶53 Effect on Estates Generally

Estate income tax rates.—The income tax rates and bracket amounts for estates and trusts are modified for tax years 2018 through 2025. The temporary tax rates are 10, 24, 35, and 37 percent.

Estate, gift, and generation-skipping transfer tax.—The basic exclusion amount for purposes of federal estate and gift taxes and the exemption amount for purposes of the generation-skipping transfer (GST) tax is doubled from $5 million to $10 million, before adjustment for inflation, for the estates of decedents dying and gifts and generation-skipping transfers made after 2017 and before 2026.

¶60 Effect on Commuters

Bicycle commuting expenses.—After December 31, 2017, and before January 1, 2026, taxpayers are not permitted to exclude any amount from their income for qualified bicycle commuting reimbursements.

¶75 Effect on Native Americans

Alaska Native settlement trusts.—New rules have been enacted to establish the tax treatment of payments received by Alaska Native Corporations and transfers made to Alaska Native Settlement Trusts.

¶78 Effect on Divorced Persons

Alimony and separate maintenance payments.—The deduction for alimony and separate maintenance payments, as well as the inclusion of the payments in gross income, are repealed. The repeal, however, is only effective for divorce or separation instruments executed or modified after 2018.

¶80 Effect on Farmers

Depreciation.—New farming machinery and equipment placed in service after December 31, 2017 are classified as 5-year MACRS property rather than 7-year MACRS property. The 7-year property classification, however, continues to apply to grain bins, cotton ginning assets, and fences.

Citrus plants.—The special rule for deducting the costs incurred in connection with replanting citrus plants lost by reason of casualty is modified. The modified rule allows for a deduction in certain instances when the cost is incurred by a person other than the taxpayer.

¶82 Effect on Virtual Currency

Like-kind exchanges.—Like-kind exchanges are allowed only for real property after 2017. Thus, as under current law, no gain or loss is recognized on the exchange of real property held for productive use in a trade or business or for investment if that real property is exchanged solely for real property of like kind that will be held either for productive use in a trade or business or for investment. Like-kind exchanges are not allowed for depreciable tangible personal property, and intangible and nondepreciable personal property after 2017.

¶84 Effect on Legislators

Living expenses.—The special provision allowing Members of Congress a deduction of up to $3,000 per year of living expenses incurred while on official business in the District of Columbia is stricken.